Miracles *and* Wonders

MIRACLES *and* WONDERS

HOW GOD CHANGES HIS
NATURAL LAWS TO BENEFIT YOU

CALVIN MILLER

WARNER
Faith

An AOL Time Warner Company

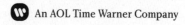 An AOL Time Warner Company

Printed in the United States of America

First Warner Books printing: March 2003

10 9 8 7 6 5 4 3 2 1

Library of Congress Control Number: 2002117223

ISBN: 0-446-53010-7

Contents

The age of miracles is forever here.
THOMAS CARLYLE

MIRACLES *and* WONDERS

Miracles: The Unpredictable God in a Predictable World

To me every hour of the dark and light is a miracle.
Every cubic inch of space is a miracle.
WALT WHITMAN

It has been said by many researchers that ninety percent of Americans believe in God and eighty percent believe in miracles. Why? It would seem we are in need of a God who is bigger than we are. We need a God behind us who can take our hopeless situations and fill them once again with hope. We want to be mystified and enthralled by a God whose every movement is larger than our problems. Give us no weak God who wants to avoid our predicament. Give us instead a God who does wonderful and impossible things—real things—miracles! We want a "pro-me" God who can—if need be—set science and logic to one side and act above such rational confines.

The Bible is the tale of such a God. This lesser book is another—a summons to a feast of miracles. My hope is that every page of it will awaken you to wonder. While you read may the lame leap. May the blind read. May the dead live once again among us.

But can such wonders come to pass? Why would God do these things? Because He is a God who is crazy about the human race and His miracles are but His way of demonstrating His love for us.

Most of us cannot conceive of Christ in any other way except in terms of His miracles. On the Friday after the Tuesday 9/11 attack on New York, I was in Newark to lead a weekend conference in a church. The results of the horrible catastrophe were everywhere obvious. The unending column of smoke continued to pour from the ruins, darkening the skies over Ellis Island. The general mood was morose. The New York area was in pain. But one little girl I met seemed an exception to the rule. She drew a picture while I preached the Sunday morning sermon and gave me her drawing after the service. It was a picture of Jesus—a gargantuan Christ—standing slightly behind and towering over the blazing skyscrapers. In her drawing the souls of those lost were flying up out of the smoke and into the waiting arms of Christ.

Where had this little artist gotten such a rich definition of Jesus? From our common perception in the West of who He is. We trust that Jesus saves our worst moments of desperation by doing something so wonderful and unexplainable that by common consent we call Him the Miracle Worker. It's a reasonable way to think of Jesus. After all, who would want a Christ who was powerless to baffle us with His irrational, outrageous love? I constantly feel my own weaknesses each time I come up against the harshness of life. I want a Jesus who can save the day precisely because He can salvage things like 9/11. Jesus must be visualized in just this way. We must be able to count on Him for a miracle when nothing else can be done.

The Double Gift of Miracles

Jesus' miracles offer us a double gift. First, they assure us of God's presence in my world. And second, they bestow upon us the gift of mystery. When life moves along in ordinary ways I find I become an ordinary, complacent person, expecting nothing extraordinary to happen. Only when my days are punctuated by the wonderful things I can't understand do I sit up and take notice. Miracles create within me a vast appetite for God's presence by feeding me a wonder that devours the ordinary. Miracles obliterate the mundane. Suddenly, *dull* isn't there anymore. God has acted. Light explodes, darkness is gone. If I then go on living a dull life after God acts, it is because I *agree* to be dull.

The poor especially need a vision of God to overcome their sense of powerlessness in a world in which they have not the means to "buy their way out of their difficulties." In 2001 Denzel Washington starred in the film *John Q,* which dealt with a poor family whose son needed a heart transplant. The film created an instant furor throughout the medical community. Most physicians and health industry experts agreed with the film—in America the best medicine is most available to those who can afford it. Hearts—and other organs—are for purchase to those with the means.

Planet Earth has always been a needy address. From the age of Christ until recent times in the West the human life span was twenty-seven years. A fourth of all babies died before their fifth birthday in seventeenth-century England, and half of all children never survived mid-adolescence. Jane Austen died in her late thirties. Shakespeare and Cervantes in their mid-fifties.

Throughout most of Western history, doctors were few. Hospitals were nonexistent before the eighteenth century. What medical help there was, was rarely accessible to the lower classes. The poor had nowhere to go each time the plague swept through Europe, often killing a third of the populace. Inoculations and vaccinations were unknown. To be infected with any disease was to die.

Miracles back then were the great hope of the masses—their only way around the hazards of existence. In the absence of medicine the poor had no door to knock on except the gates of God. But God was God! He could amend the usual order of things as He wished. Explainable wonder held little healing for the people's desperation. When there was no logical way out, they needed a kind of medicine too wonderful for logic. Miracles were seen to be God's method and mystery was the wrapping in which He packaged them.

Natural law is our celebration of the reliability of God. It is the signature of God on explainable wonder. How nice to have a dawn once every twenty-four hours. But such predictability has for its chief flaw the fact that it is predictable, and *predictable* does not fascinate. Mystery does.

And the mystery behind all miracles takes away our feelings of powerlessness in a desperate world. When God's miracle and mystery sweep into human hopelessness the crippled win marathons. The slow of wit join the Mensa Society. The hungry eat by the thousands. Life becomes exciting because God has gotten involved in our seemingly petty days. Suddenly we can see that God has not abandoned us to a heartless, boring world to manage on our own. *Immanuel!* "He is with us."

Routine be done with!

Boring begone!

We, the "little" people of the planet who thought our broken world could not be mended, are not so powerless after all. Our tears matter and God's miracles have come to end our crying. As I said before, the poor have always been needy. And so it is to the poor that miracles often come.

Recently in Nassau I was touched by the great disparity between the rich and poor. After lunching in the resplendent Atlantis Hotel, I walked the streets of Nassau. At the big hotels, secular jazz rolled on for those who could afford it. Sweet but empty notes! It was in the tiny shops and cabs on the back streets that I heard the sounds of gospel music. There the poor lived and depended on God for their hope. They knew from whence came their help, and they celebrated it.

Cookie Bakke had such an experience as mine in Nigeria. She said that a certain Mr. Coomsie, a Nigerian cab driver, told her that—after losing a better job—taking a job as a cab driver was the hardest thing he had ever done. It had forced him to take two or his three children out of school because he could no longer afford their tuition. Mrs. Bakke asked him how much the tuition was.

He told her it cost eight hundred naira, a sum equal to ten American dollars.

Mrs. Bakke opened her purse, took out a business card and a U.S. twenty-dollar bill, and handed them to him.

"Please put your other two children back into school," she said, "and write to me when it is time to again pay their tuition and I will help you."

Suddenly the driver's eyes rolled upward and he began to mumble in an unintelligible stream of words, "I know that Jesus has sent you here to Nigeria to answer my prayers. I know you are a messenger for Jesus."[1]

Again, he knew from whence came his help.

You will find as you read these pages an emphasis on miracles that may seem to you to lack the grandeur of those Israel experienced during the Exodus. But sometimes "little" people of this world need only little miracles to waken them to praise. But it is gallant praise—the unstoppable flood of joy from the emotionally destitute who have seen God sweep away the confining tedium of their world.

In Greco-Roman mythology there lived a man named Sysiphus. For angering the gods he was sentenced to the most meaningless kind of hell imaginable. He was condemned each day to roll a huge stone up a high mountain. When his long, soul-destroying struggle finally ended at the top of the incline, he was ordered to let it roll back down the mountain. Then the gods commanded him to follow it back down and then roll it up again the next day, and so on for eternity. Sysiphus' tale is a story of meandering drudgery. His life had no purpose. It was an endless cycle of empty routine.

But the myth of Sysiphus is no myth. Sysiphus is us. Sysiphus is now. He is a worker in an automobile plant ordered to put the same door latch on five hundred cars a week, week after week, year after year. Such a person's life is a living hell. And hell, as *The Singer* said, is a place "where you have nothing to look back upon with pride, and nothing to look forward to with hope." The only escape many of us have from our forty-hour-a-week hell is to go home at night, crash in front of the TV, and pray that the morning is further away than the alarm clock will make it seem.

The only antidote to such pointless drudgery is mystery. We cannot live without it. Nor do we want to live without the miracles that come packaged in mystery. We of the computer age swelter under a glut of information. We've had too many things explained to us. We need a fresh encounter with things that can't be explained. In Christ we come face-to-face with a force in the universe that exists to do unexplainable things in our lives and we must feel that force.

Perhaps that is why we Christians often put a little more "oomph" in our testimony than is necessary. I knew an old man once who explained his late-life conversion in terms of that force. He said that when he got "saved" it felt "like squirrels running up and down his back." We often describe our affairs with God in some such sensate fashion. I have often described my own post-conversion euphoria in the words of the Czech novelist Milan Kundera as "the unbearable lightness of being." I have another friend who says that when he came to Christ the "inner dam of all his sins burst instantly forth and his flood of joy was unimaginable." If John Bunyan is speaking for himself in *Pilgrim's Progress,* he spoke of his salvation as feeling the great burden of his sin "roll off his shoulders and down, down, down . . . into the mouth of the open tomb."

Why do we offer such dramatic descriptions of our own coming to Christ? Perhaps because we are only trying to reckon with the notion that our affair with the God of miracle must be more mysterious than matter-of-fact. Without such a mystery we seem only gnats in the giant machinery of an unexplainable universe. Such feelings of triviality not only diminish us, they deny us the right to be made in the image of God and to see ourselves as his special friends.

Remember the game *Trivial Pursuit*? Triviality is no game. It is a nightmare. There is nothing more tedious than the pointless pursuit of the trivial. Who would want to pursue it? To try to chase it down is to have it nibble at our significance, destroying our self-esteem. That powerless feeling that we don't matter dogs our days. We read of the rich and famous—movie stars and the like—who live grand lives. But their lives are not ours. We do the laundry. We gas up the car, dry the dishes, and it is morning once again.

Then the God of miracles enters our tedium and the trivial import of our lives is set to soaring. As God's importance grows in us, we grow, too. When we see His miracles, we believe He is God. In the film the *Ten Commandments*, Pharaoh beholds the Red Sea split and cries of Moses: "His God is God." Great miracles leave us with no other conclusion.

Miracle and mystery: unsolvable and glorious! Without miracles we have no meaning in our lives. Unless we encounter truth deeper than our minds can plumb, we must live out our days caged in our own boring, explainable world. Oh, we may from time to time think we would like to understand more of God. Not so! Give us no God whom we can chart or measure. Such a God is no God at all. Only a mind-boggling God is Almighty enough to be of any use to us.

A few years ago my fascination with Theresa of Avila and John of the Cross led me to stand outside a Spanish cave in Avila to ponder all that supposedly occurred there. It is said that when these sixteenth-century saints prayed in that cave, their fervor for God was so intense they levitated even as they prayed. My enthusiasm to enter this cave led me to crack my head on the low stone lintel of the cave as I entered. The blow was so severe it nearly staggered me. My wife said that I deserved it for being so credulous about local superstitions. Perhaps she is right. But I could not deny my eagerness to see the place where the great mysteries of God "perhaps" unfolded. I sought a God I could not understand—a God who could convince me of His relevance. I will serve no God who cannot overcome my tedium with terror and baffle me with mystery.

Miracles, the Terror of Mystery

Thomas Jefferson, during his term of office, rewrote the New Testament by excising the passages he didn't agree with. Most of these had to do with Jesus' miracles, which Jefferson couldn't accept. Only in 1904 (a hundred years after the fact) was Jefferson's work published. It has for the past century been deemed the Jefferson Bible, and with some reluctance I purchased a copy of it recently. Jefferson—a Deist—would have nothing to do with faith in the biblical Christ. What a poor exchange, to barter the Christ of miracles for the Christ of philosophy. Jefferson left Christ smaller than he was.

Yet we know Christ of Christianity is more than the sum of His sermons. He is an "awesome" Christ—the terrible and wondrous God-man. He is not Christ the namby-pamby founder of a new world "ism." He is Christ the Tiger teaching us the wonder and terror of the Almighty. To feel this terror is to confess that I am a child, afraid of what I cannot understand. Yet terror titillates me. I want to be terrified as much as I don't. I want to brag that I survived the rafting of the most horrible river or my ride on the world's highest roller coaster. Only when I have felt the terror can I claim the joy and the meaning I found in conquering it. Then having conquered it I am then free to experience God's miracles.

"This is our miracle baby," a couple once told me of their child just before the baby was to be dedicated in a public ceremony.

"Why 'miracle'?" I asked.

"Because the doctor told us our child would not survive birth. But we prayed and, as you can see, we now possess our own little miracle of God."

I could see. But I saw more than a miracle, I saw that the soil of this miracle was the couple's absolute need for God to quit being entirely nonpartisan and come through just for them. He did. And at the very place where their need met God's supply a miracle was born.

In an odd sense this is why I too need the God of miracles. He is the God who jellies my fear into self-confidence. I call out to Him over the waves, "Lord, if it is you, bid me come to you on the water." Then suddenly I find myself out of the boat. I am standing on Galilee. The hair rises on my neck. I am being "miraclized" by the terror of doing impossible things. God is aroar all about me.

It is an awe-inspiring moment. It is as if I am at the highest ascent of a roller coaster. I am about to plunge into an abyss of fear. But for the moment the roller coaster tram freezes in time and I meditate on the terror soon to fall upon me. Existence seems to stop. All is surreal. I look around at the lofty world I so lately contemplated from the ground.

Then I plunge, plunge, plunge! My heart is in my throat. Can these flying rails be stopped? Can the horrible war in the pit of my stomach be called to peace? Will I survive the g-force that is tearing me from the straps and pouring white into my knuckles? Who knows? But I must embrace the experience. Why? Because all titanic mystery gives us life.

When my wife and I first moved to Kansas City as newlyweds, our tiny third-floor apartment was invaded one night by a sleepwalker. It occurred around two A.M. when we were both sleeping soundly. When I woke, I saw in the dark interior of our bedroom a "filmy white" person who appeared at first glance to be a ghost. My eye sifted the thick gloom of our garret flat trying to fathom the exact form of this poltergeist. The filmy intruder behaved most erratically. For a while, this tottering nightstalker, tall and threatening, stood immobile in the center of the room. Then it walked over and stood at the foot of our bed. Now I was really terrified! I shook my wife awake and pointing to the specter."What is that?"

She sat straight up in bed. "Esther?" This was the name of the girl who lived in the apartment just below us.

"Whhhattt?" Esther replied groggily.

How glad I was that this willowy specter could be identified and explained. Why? Because the things we cannot explain terrify us. Only as reason dissects our reality can we lay by our terror and return to our former world of peace.

Likewise miracles fill us with fear. How many times did the disciples back away from Jesus because He had just done something too immense for their nervous systems to handle? They were overwhelmed by fear and wonder, and why wouldn't they be? Jesus had stilled the storms and walked on water. He terrified them with mystery. Yet this was a terror they craved.

No wonder F.W. Faber wrote:

They love Thee little if at all/who do not fear Thee much,/If love is Thine attraction Lord,/fear is thy very touch.

God has the power to make our flesh crawl and our spines tingle. Jesus' miracles make our hair stand on end and our hearts stand at attention. Something powerful and unstoppable is before us and we had better agree to it or be crushed by its eerie reality.

Only The God of the Unbelievable Is God

We are ever being overwhelmed by all that science lays before us. As Eric Hofer once said, our current addiction to technology is "our banging on the gates of Eden!" We want back into paradise and we believe science can give us the gadgets that will swing wide those long-locked gates. The technology itself is not miraculous but it has brought a sense of miracle near. Technology's "miracles" have made toast from bread and flight from fossil fuels. But those who have felt the sheer terror of real miracles know it is a poor trade.

Thomas Merton broadened Hofer's view of paradise revisited when he said that Jesus' miracle of changing water into wine was really a "wine for old Adam, digging in the briars outside of Eden." He pictures the wedding reception this way:

> For Jesus came, and His Disciples, and His mother,
> And after them the singers and some men with violins . . .
> Nor did we seem to fear the wine would fail:
> For reading, in a row, to fill with water and a miracle,
> We saw our earthen vessels, waiting empty.
> What wine those humble water jars foretell!"[2]

We are such jars, too full of ordinary water to be anything more than ordinary. We want to be filled with something more intoxicating. We want our watery plainness to change. We are the water, too—begging God to change our aqueous lives into the wine of more inebriated and heady living!

Imagine the man with a withered hand who met Jesus. Having made millions of good hands Jesus understood the pain of this poor man. Then Jesus spoke. The withered hand was well. Suddenly the terror of his miracle was swallowed up in the delirium of this man's new and glorious health. As Amos Wells's carpenter cried out, "I am a man, no more a burdened cumberer! Give me a hammer and any piece of wood."

But as wondrous as physical healing may be, spiritual healing is far greater. Conversion is the grandest miracle of all. I know this miracle. I was once the bland, plain water untouched by mystery. But I have been made new. I am the water changed to wine. I am well. Like the man with the withered hand I have arrived at a new and glorious sense of my significance. I have come to know who I am and why I was created in the first place.

Jesus did not heal all the sick of His day. When He came the world was sick. It was still sick after He left it. But health is illusory. Even the most robust are never completely well. The big miracle is not in having someone make us entirely well, but the ability to see ourselves that way.

Don Quixote was the first modern novel. Cervantes's lanky knight is a Christ symbol who spends himself in creating miracles of self-worth. Aldonza, his "lady," is not healed of anything except her devalued way of seeing herself. Quixote gives her grace—a better way of seeing herself. In a similar way Jesus touched me, supplied me with grace. I got well. After knowing Christ I left the ranks of those who struggle with low self-esteem. I have been set free to live on a higher plane.

I once knew a withered woman. Twice withered she was: her soul had shriveled up before her fear of people because she had to learn to live with a withered leg. As a young woman, polio had taken the use of her leg. Until the paralysis overtook her, she confessed, she had been most self-sufficient. She was then a beautiful, young woman caught up in the selfish dreams of late adolescence. She had set her heart on becoming a concert pianist. She dreamed of nothing else but thrilling people with her vast musical talent.

Enter polio!

This woman promised God that if He would leave her two good hands and one good leg she would dedicate her talent to Him for the rest of her life. And so God healed her and held her to her bargain. Suddenly her life became a self-declarative miracle. She was not made completely whole and remained a cripple for the rest of her life; her left leg was forever braced. But in leaving her a bit of her disease, God made her music accessible to all of us.

There are all kinds of miracles. Some miracles take away our overdone self-confidence to make us useful to God. Others add to it to make us useful. Becoming a believer is the most widespread evidence of miracle. We the dying hopeless were touched by an outside power and changed from mortals to immortals. Why should I refuse to believe in miracles: my entire life with God is the stamp of miracle. Being visited by this great wonder, my mortalness is clothed with immortality and all things perishable have dressed themselves with permanence (1 Corinthians 15:53-ff).

Miracles and Intoxicated Living

Miracles are addicting. They hold an intoxication all their own.

Nehemiah was a cupbearer. He it was who first drank from the King's cup so the King could be sure that none had poisoned him. Can you imagine the sheer terror and joy of such a job? Here came the king's wine. "Have a sip, Nehemiah. If you live, then I'll drink it," said the king. So Nehemiah lifted the cup. What would be the outcome? Would he smile and lick his lips with delight, or would he fall to the floor clutching his throat? Who could say? The king had lots of enemies, so no single cup of wine could ever be tasted in a casual manner. So Nehemiah lived with the terror and joy of his calling. Gulp! Eureka! No poison!

As Nehemiah could surely attest, such fear and wonder are never boring. Ray Bradbury's *Dandelion Wine* tells the tale of a "bogey man" who lived in the horrible night grove and stalked those casual citizens who thought they would chance taking a shortcut through the woods late at night. They were inevitably stalked by this sinister ripper. Sometimes he succeeded. Sometimes he didn't. But one day the night-stalker was killed. The town became very safe after his death, but it was never very interesting. Nothing is more boring than safety. So, once the ogre was dead, the town had to learn to live without the fear and trembling that once heightened their existence.

I happened to be on the campus of Oral Roberts University some years ago when the evangelist and healer had his 'vision of a 900 foot Jesus.' It was on the front of every newspaper across America, and certainly all Tulsa was abuzz with excitement regarding the gargantuan Jesus who had come to Oral's life.

I was speaking in chapel that day and so I felt some necessity of referring to the vision since it was so much on everyone's mind. I was there to speak on the inner life in Christ so I opened my sermon by saying, "Your chancellor has had a vision of a Christ of three hundred meters [it didn't sound so overwhelming in the metric system]. But I would like to invite your attention to the 'thumbnail Christ' of Theresa of Avila who sits on the throne of the believing heart, demanding your allegiance." I went on from there to talk about the Christ of obedience and mystery.

While I thought Oral's view of Jesus was a bit titanic, I felt that most people I knew were suffering from absolutely no vision of Jesus. We have so domesticated our Lord that he is capable of little more than going to Sunday School. We sing and preach about him, but he is really too much like us to help us. There is too little power left in the church-broken Jesus to terrify us. He's never outlandish. He's a drowsy messiah indeed.

Will we long abide a Jesus who never inspires us to anything risky?

I think not.

To become God's child is to risk and hazard all we have. Garner this great miracle to yourself and own God's wonder in the center of your soul.

At the center of this book is a core group of thirty-two contemporary miracles. I haven't numbered them but I have let them stand enmeshed in my attempt to show that miracles still happen. I have also leaned on Jesus' thirty-five recorded miracles as well as many of those wonders that dominate the Old Testament. In some sections of this book (namely chapters three and four) I have sought to show how essential Jesus' own recorded miracles are to our understanding and acceptance of miracles. So every paragraph of this book is set forth to make real the involvement of God in the miracles of the Bible as well as those in our own time. A miracle in any age is an occasion to remember God acts in ways that baffle us to demonstrate his reality. He is real. So are his acts. So is our need to be mystified with deeds too large for our small hearts.

CHAPTER ONE

Miracles: The Mysterious Force of Faith

Water in His presence must be wine or be ashamed.
At Cana of Galilee
"The conscious water knew its Lord and blushed."
RICHARD CRASHAW

Logic is the foundation of knowledge but miracles are the foundation of faith. Only when a dead man lives again is there any point in believing.

But why are the miracles of Christ so much more believable than those we see on cable television? TV miracles seem more entertaining than transforming. They seem so instant and unverifiable. So commercial. So much an ad campaign for the undiscovered God. They leave us hungry for a more certain view of Him. We all want a little less, "Brother, thou art healed—put something in the plate," and a little more, "Rise, take up your bed and walk."

All miracles—contemporary or otherwise—take interpretation. For instance, I know Jesus multiplied loaves; I accept this without question. But I remember a woman who invited thirty-five people to her home, forgetting she had only one small churn of homemade ice cream to feed them. According to her, she laid hands on her churn, blessed it, and miraculously fed them all with much to spare.

Why do I believe Jesus' multiplication of the loaves and not her multiplication of the quarts? Because . . . well, to be honest, she seemed a bit "off-the-wall" to me. But frankly it just seems that multiplying loaves and fishes is more biblical than multiplying ice cream. Most of us have a natural prejudice in favor of biblical miracles. Television miracles seem smaller and less trustworthy than those of Scripture. Perhaps the things I classify as miracles in my own life are in some cases less showy than asking God to multiply ice cream.

Contemporary miracles rarely come in biblical proportions. For years my wife and I made an annual hike through the Grand Canyon. The hike was a simple matter of leaving the South Rim, following the Kaibab Trail down to the Colorado River, staying all night at the Phantom Ranch, and hiking back up the Bright Angel Trail to arrive once again on the South Rim of the Canyon. The climb back to the surface was always a kind of exhilarating agony.

On one of our trips to the canyon we decided to park our car on the South Rim, take a bus around to the North Rim, and hike down through and across the canyon. While the cross-canyon trip is only twenty-eight miles, the trip around the canyon to the north trailhead is 180 miles. Nonetheless we made the trip and began our hike down into the canyon.

During that ill-fated hike we both became terribly sick with heat exhaustion. Dehydrated and vomiting profusely, we weren't sure we'd be able to reach sanctuary at the Phantom Ranch on the banks of the Colorado River on the floor of the canyon. Even if we did, we felt we could not make it through the night in the dormitories where we usually stayed. So I began to pray that we would be able to have one of the private cabins in which to spend the night. These units are few in number and nearly always given to those who pay a premium excursion fare to ride the mules to the bottom. In all my previous years of trying I had never been able to secure one of them.

Now throughout my years of praying I have rarely asked God to do anything for me personally. I believe prayer counts most when we are able to get others to pray for us or when we pray for others. But on this occasion I actually asked God to give us one of those private cabins for our much needed rest. And, as I'm sure you've surmised, when we reached the bottom of the canyon there was a cabin available. God blessed us what we asked for and our violent illness was much more bearable than it would have been in the dormitories.

Should I use the word *miracle* to refer to this? I believe so. Miracles come in all sizes. While this miracle seems small indeed when placed alongside the crossing of the Red Sea in Exodus, I nonetheless found the compassion of God in His direct reply to our desperation.

It is an interesting paradox. All of us both crave and doubt miracles. We receive them yet often fail to believe them because they seem so much smaller than Bible-sized miracles.

Once a man from my church went to an Oklahoma cable-TV faith healer to be delivered from cataracts. He was healed and came back seeing. Of course, his new sight was a terrible inconvenience to his ophthalmologist who would have preferred the man call up a surgeon. And, if I'm honest with myself, I guess I was a bit perturbed as well. Perhaps, deep down, I too wished the man would have gone on a pilgrimage to Lourdes or consulted a miracle worker with a little more class. But the man had regained his sight and his miracle was one we all had to live with—television evangelist or not. Which brings us to another challenge of miracles.

Three Responses to Miracle

Not only are we beset with the problem of whether miracles really happen, but we must forever struggle with our response to them. Ours is an age hungry for the unexplainable benevolence of God. Yet we want every miracle to undergo the strictest of spiritual forensics so we can be sure it happened even as the "miracle-ized" say it did. We believe, but we want to be sure some credible witness has signed on the bottom line that she actually saw the whole thing happen.

There are a lot of responses to miracles, but here are my three favorites:

1. Do That Again!

I call this the Houdini Response. It's how audiences reply to an illusionist. When Mr. Copperfield makes the Statue of Liberty disappear we all know it's a trick, but we want him to do it again. Why? So we can watch very carefully the second time. Houdini would have had the same effect on Herod that Jesus did. In *Jesus Christ Superstar* Herod sings to Jesus, "Prove to me that you're real cool. Walk across my swimming pool!" Herod wanted some evidence up front. To the poor deluded King of Judea, Jesus was only a high-quality illusionist, the Nazarene Houdini of His day.

2. Wow!

This response to miracle is but the "oohing and aahing" of reactionary believing. The reaction is positive in that it doesn't seek to figure out how the miracle was done. But neither is the "ooher" or "ahher" changed by the miracle. The magicians of Egypt, like Moses, could create snakes from sticks. It was a good show for everybody, but the Exodus did not begin with a stick-to-snake miracle. The miracle that changed history was not a miracle that merely wowed the crowd. It was the killing Passover miracle that forced Egypt to make a decision about God's demands.

Likewise, there were plenty of people ready to follow Jesus after the feeding of the five thousand. But when Jesus invited them to a more difficult communion than that of bread and fish, the crowd fell away. Jesus' call was a call to blood and death—the cost of discipleship. "Come with me and die" was a miracle of discipline they could not bear.

3. Lord, I Believe.

This is the best response to miracles. Thomas the Doubter didn't believe the resurrection until he actually saw the Lord alive again. Yet when he saw the living Christ, he didn't just say, "Oh, now I see." What he came to believe was not the miracle itself, but the Christ behind the miracle. This is the best result of miracles. To believe in Christ is more than being either curious or wowed. It is to commit ourselves to the God of the Bible and to Jesus Christ His only Son. Jesus testified to this when He said, after healing the blind man, "Neither this man nor his parents sinned that he was born blind, but that the power of God might be made manifest in his body" (John 9:4). The mightiest of wonders cause people to not believe in them but in the God who accomplishes them.

The Ones That Get Away

But, you may be thinking, what of the times I have prayed for a miracle and yet God didn't come through for me? How can such an obvious shortcoming in the Almighty induce me to believe in Him?

I once traveled on a very small commuter plane through a very large storm. A man sitting beside me actually died during that flight. He had a heart attack. I watched him dealing with death as our tiny plane was tossed from thunderhead to thunderhead. Amidst the tumult and roaring, I tried without success to get the pilot's attention (I dared not loosen my own seat belt to try to move forward to the cockpit). By the time I finally managed to notify the captain, it was too late. The pilot radioed ahead for an ambulance and paramedics; when we actually reached the runway the poor man was dead.

My prayers for a miracle were unavailing. But, then, we must remember miracles are kept in the vaults of heaven. Sometimes we ask and God answers with fire and our needs meet his supply. But sometimes we pray and our desperation seems not to reach God's rich deposit of miracles. Our physical needs do not always end in miracle. A miracle may take a thirty-year life and extend it into an eighty-year life. But nobody goes on being healed indefinitely. None slip past God's great deadline of Hebrews 9:27: "It is appointed unto man once to die."

But our puny lifespans cannot devour the glory of our final reward in heaven. Heaven is the greatest of miracles. The glory of immortality will at last obliterate all our seemingly unanswered prayers for health. Paul reminded us that the sufferings of the present time do not outweigh the glory that shall be (Romans 8:18). Just how temporary is it? If you could plot all the years of your life on a giant clock so that each hour of that clock equaled six years of your life, you could understand how fleeting your life is and how great is the miracle of heaven. If you were to plot all of your years on such a clock where you were born at eight o'clock in the morning and died at eight o'clock in the evening, every hour of that clock would consume six years of your life. At nine o'clock you would be six and you would die at eight that evening. At ten o'clock you would be twelve. At one o'clock you would be thirty. And so on. It is easy to see why Job said we are like "straw before the wind" (Job 21:18). It is easy to see why James called his life a wisp of smoke in a driving wind (see James 4:14).

During the time I was writing this book, my father-in-law died and I officiated at his funeral. I can hardly relate the emotional impact this funeral had upon me. All of my relatives are buried in that same cemetery where my wife's father was laid to rest and all of our burial plots as you might expect are within inches of each other. I own the cemetery plot next to my father-in-law's. I actually stood on my own cemetery plot to conduct "Daddy's" committal service. The dirt from his grave was piled on my plot. It was a chilling omen.

As I preached that funeral I felt an odd emotion. I looked out at my family all of whom are older than I (and I am no longer young). For one moment, it seemed, I thought I was a skeleton, speaking my father-in-law's eulogy to a whole crowd of skeletons. I was in Ezekiel's valley of dry bones. I realized it would not be long before I myself was in a box, with someone else standing beside that box to read the same kinds of words over me.

Life is brief and I am counting on the miracle of heaven to extend it. Without that miracle, my life would end with no assurance. In short I am miracle-dependent. But I am among those who are counting on the miracle of resurrection. It is this miracle that makes of death only an inconvenience in the path to heaven, the greatest miracle of all.

Why Are Miracles a Must?

Miracles are a must because without them I can live at best only a plain life where I am locked for my three-score-and-ten years in a vault called the Laws of Nature. These laws were not established to undo me. In fact they make my life possible. Because of the laws of nature I may expect and even predict tomorrow's sunrise. Because of those laws I know that the designer of the *Titanic* bragged foolishly of its unsinkable status. Because of these laws I understand why the *Hindenburg* crashed.

Once, when Francis Schaeffer was crossing the Atlantic by air, he noticed (somewhere at mid-crossing) that the airplane seemed to be losing altitude. Dr. Schaeffer said that after a while he began praying that the rapidly sinking flight "would be healed." When it was close enough to the water that other passengers began to express alarm, Dr. Schaeffer's prayers "locked in" and there was a sudden lurch of the aircraft as it began once again to regain the lost altitude.

When they arrived in New York, Dr. Schaeffer related to the pilot his prayers with the question, "Do you believe prayer can reignite a cold engine?" The pilot only smiled, as if he'd been found out.

The laws of physics must be honored for they are hard fast rules. But a single praying passenger may abrogate the force of physics and chemistry and order the world back to honoring God's interruption of natural law. So, miracles assure us that the unbending laws of science are not free to condemn us to their hard conclusions. God on His own—at His caprice—can speak to all the maxims of science and place His own demands on those laws.

Most men have a fear of having their physician say, "I'm sorry, but you have pancreatic cancer." Why? Because pancreatic cancer is almost always 100 percent fatal. To have it is to know you will most likely die. In spite of the Houston Clinic, people who have it die. It is a law of nature, a dreaded truth bolted beneath the hasp of scientific law that always has its way.

I have known only a few men who faced this horrible killer. They all died. The ardent faith of their families and friends did not avail. My prayers as their pastor could not save them. I have seen other kinds of cancer healed, but never this kind. In my experience this one law of nature—so far—has never been annulled.

Will this always be the case? Has this particular cancer ever been healed by a miracle? Who can say? This is the beauty of miracle. Somewhere, at some time, every condemning scientific mandate has been beaten back by that great overcomer called *miracle*. There will likely be in heaven with me some who beat pancreatic cancer and are only in heaven because they died of some other cause. Such a victor will testify "This particular law of nature did not apply to me. In me, God set aside that rule to show me that neither He nor I was imprisoned in a system of laws. Marvel not! God is not bound up in a cold and harsh legal system of His own making. There is always hope."

Paul Gallico wrote a novel called *The Snow Goose*. The story finds its fascination with an event in history called the Miracle of

Dunkirk. In that miracle the British Army in World War I was trapped on European soil, where they were being eradicated by the enemy, whose artillery had pounded them unmercifully to the shores of the North Sea. Then, in response to the prayers of English wives and mothers, a great fog fell over the battle. Under this shielding reprieve all the English who had seaworthy boats and vessels of any sort sailed to the mainland and platoon by platoon rescued the endangered army. Fishers, eelers, freighters, motorized barges—all crossed the stormy channel and saved the British army.

One of those who responded was a lighthouse keeper, whose physical deformities had kept him from enlisting in the army. The odd miracle of that night allowed him to sail his little skiff, rescue soldiers, and bring them safely home to England. This lighthouse keeper had once befriended a wing-broken snow goose, which he had rescued and healed. This bird flew like an angel to guide the ships' pilot through a frantic, foggy night of miracle.

Could a snow goose have been a helper in England's greatest and most national miracle? Who's to say? But the story exists to remind us that the things we cannot understand are the things that supply us the mystery, without which meaningful living is impossible. God loves us too much to leave us locked in a cruel system of laws.

Britain experienced an earlier miracle in 1588 when the "invincible" Spanish Armada came to restore Catholicism to England. It is said that the desperate English prayed for God to help them repulse the overwhelming Spanish fleet that flooded the Thames River. In response to their prayers there came the famed "Protestant Wind," which filled the sails of the English ships and allowed them to attack the Armada. Because of the direction of the wind, the Spanish galleons could not tack against the limp sails of their cause, and they were unable to advance. The British won the day.

Although the English considered the wind a miracle, the Spanish of course did not. There is after all no miracle that is miraculous for everyone. But it did appear to the English that the God of gales was on their side.

Shakespeare had his beleaguered Henry V cry after the Battle of Agincourt, *"Non nobis, Domine!* Oh God, thine arm was here: And not to us, but to thine arm alone, ascribe we all!"[3] In how many of our own little victories do we shout in joy for our own outcomes, "Our God fought for us"?

Miracles make us ever more aware that God acts on behalf of His children by setting aside the laws of nature to benefit His children. Isn't that what He did at the Red Sea? The open tomb? He set aside the way things usually work because the way things usually work was of no value to Him in His love affair with those of us who need the redeeming joy of His mysteries. He continues to do so today. They might not be as prominent or significant as some miracles of old. They might not happen in such obvious ways. But they do happen!

The Miracle of Being On Time

Marjorie Kimbrough tells of a girl named Lucy who was on her way home from a day of teaching in Alameda, California, on October 17, 1989. Ordinarily she took the Nimitz Freeway to her home in El Cerrito, but as she was about to enter the freeway ramp she had the distinct impression that she should not continue. Suddenly her car began to shake and so she pulled to a stop believing that she might have had a flat tire. As she got out of her car to inspect the tires, she saw many other motorists doing the same thing.

It was not a flat tire, it was an earthquake and in a moment she heard the deafening roar of the collapse of the Nimitz Freeway. The super road buckled into concrete shards and the entire multi-laned bridge collapsed killing forty-two people and trapping and wounding several more. Had Lucy taken the Nimitz she would have doubtlessly died in an earthquake that registered 7.1 on the Richter scale.[4]

The laws of nature were very explicit that October afternoon. There was a law that relates to tectonic plates scraping against each other at Richter 7.1. There was another law that related to the tensile strength of the concrete reinforcing rods that ran through the doomed section of freeway. There were laws relating to gravity and collapsing concrete. Had Lucy outsmarted those laws? Not at all, but she was obedient to an inner voice that brought her an escape from death. This miracle is largely a mir-acle of timeliness. Lucy escaped injury or death because she was obedient in some mysterious sense to God's timing.

There are times when God does not set aside a law of nature, but allows us instead to beat the clock. I once had a woman in our congregation who was dying of a heart condition that could be remedied only if she could find a suitable donor to supply her a heart. But, alas, no suitable donor could be found. She was finally at death's door and the family had been called in so she could take her farewells of them all. Being pastor, I arrived at the hospital with one of our associate pastors and went in to say a prayer for her as she left the world at hand, performing what Baptists might called last rites. In my prayer for her I asked the Lord to heal her and make her well.

Upon leaving her, the associate pastor who was with me rebuked me sharply saying, "Do you really think it's wise to pray for her healing when this woman is clearly beyond all hope?"

"There is always hope," I replied. "It is a practice of mine always to extend hope. I never leave a sick person without praying for Christ to heal them. Not to pray for a friend is to waver in trust for what we really want God to do for them. Not to ask from God what we really want abandons our faith to dismal acceptance and despair. And you are wrong. Hope is the hallmark of faith. In Christ we are ever to remember the empty tomb and claim the victory: there is always hope!"

That very night, a young man died in an auto accident in a city one hundred miles distant. His heart was flown directly from his thorax to my friend's, and six weeks later she was back in church and in the pulpit giving glory to God for the miracle He had provided her. In her case no law of nature had been suspended; it was a miracle of timing, but a miracle nonetheless. And one in which our whole church exulted.

Of course, we must remember a young man died in a tragedy that plunged his family into unutterable loss, so that a woman in our church could lay claim to a miracle of God. As I said earlier, tragedy and miracle all point to the issue of interpretation. Was the heart transplant a miracle or a tragedy? It depends upon whether you were a recipient or a donor, of course. But, then, the same thing is true of the incident with Moses at the Red Sea. Was this really a miracle of God? It depends upon whether you were an Israeli or an Egyptian. So many lives were lost in Egypt through this act of God that Pharaoh never called it a miracle.

I remember the first church-building program our church endeavored to complete. The program was going poorly because the new building site was virtually a mountain that had to be excavated to make room for the new building. We were a poor little congregation with no money in hand to hire the removal of thousands of tons of earth. It looked like our dream for the project was to be lost to our inability to pay for the removal of our mountain.

Then came the horror of the unstoppable spring rains. The skies opened, swelling the angry rivers to capacity. These storms, coupled with the spring thaw in the mountains, sent the waterways of the plains into spasms of roaring rivers that made vast lakes of our rich farmland in Nebraska and Iowa. The floods devastated not only farms, but earthen dams, railroads, and rural highways and interstates. The damage ran into the millions of dollars.

During these days of misery, the highway commissioner came to me. "We hear you need a lot of earth excavated to make way for a building."

"Yes," I said. "But we'll have to wait till we have money to get it done."

"We'll excavate it for you free," he said, "in exchange for the earth we need to rebuild the devastated roads and bridge approaches in this area. Just show us the earth you want moved and we'll take it all away. It won't cost you a dime."

Our little congregation was exultant. "It is a miracle!" they cried.

"No, not altogether," I said. "For us to have this miracle, hundreds of thousands of acres of good farms and roads had to be destroyed."

It was a miracle that needed a lot of interpretation. But for us it was at least a miracle of timing. God had violated no law of nature but the timing of the great floods was at least favorable to our own small, private agenda.

Timing also played a part on the night of May 25, 2002, when my wife and I were traveling west on I-40 between Ft. Smith, Arkansas, and Oklahoma City, Oklahoma. We were tired but decided we would try to drive another fifty miles or so before trying to locate a motel room and spend the night. It seemed like we made this decision on the basis of no more than an innocent whim at the time. But shortly after we crossed the Arkansas River Waterway, a tugboat operator lost consciousness and ran his string of barges into the I-40 bridge, dislodging a bridge pier. As a result the bridge collapsed and thirteen people lost their lives. Could it have happened to us? I cannot say for sure, but had we served our first inclination and rested even for ten minutes in Ft. Smith, we might have been counted among the victims. So we gave God great praise for our safety. We were serving a timetable we couldn't have imagined. It was as though God had created another clock for us to follow.

The Mystery That Redeems Us

But we must understand the one great truth that lies at the core of miracles. Putting aside our struggle with biblical miracles or modern ones, positive or negative responses, laws of nature or simple timing, we must remember the grand interpretation for every miracle: We are not alone. We are loved. The predictable world of happenstance has fallen so clearly in our direction that we can only say, "God was here! We cannot doubt that we are loved and that God is on our side."

Miracles remind me that I must be worth something to God, for he can act in unusual and unpredictable ways to liberate me from a life of captivity. Captivity? Yes, for without miracles I remain chained to a great lie: I am all alone in life and there is no God of mighty acts who can liberate me from the laws of nature; I am but a prisoner of the dull routine of my "scientific" days in which the whole human race is held captive.

Miracle: God Set Free of His Own Laws

The philosophers have constantly spoken of Deism as *Deus Ex Machina*. The Deists state that God—whoever He is, and we can never know for sure—made the world, set up the laws of nature, and then stepped out of it to let His cosmic machine run on its own. We poor mortals have inherited this forsaken machine and are held captive in it. We are prisoners in a scientifically determined world.

Yet deists forever struggle with their own interpretation. It was said that the Marquis de Sade could argue convincingly that everything was chemically determined, even morality. By his reckoning any happenstance was therefore right and just. How odd, then, that during his confinement in Charenton Lunatic Asylum, he complained of "unjust" treatment by his jailers. If all he was was only an aggregate of chemicals, why did he not accept their treatment as logical and live by his philosophy? Why did he spend hours poring over his wife's letters? He took those letters seriously although "according to his own argument, they were just the chemical etchings of an autonomous and absurd universe. Is it possible that de Sade himself was reaching for a why for life?"[5]

Voltaire obviously felt the same when he said it was inconceivable that an infinitely wise God would make natural laws only to violate them. According to Voltaire, when God made natural law, he did so to give us the miracle of predictability. If the sun did not always come up in the East, ours would be a baffling world. Thus natural law itself is a predictable miracle that makes all life possible.

But we know differently. God must be free to supercede His natural law. We would find no meaning in a God who would shut us up in His system and walk away. But God has broken the rigid laws of nature to say, "You matter to me! You are so much more than the system. See, I have broken the inherent stupidity of life. You mean more to me more than the laws of nature in which you see yourself trapped."

Not everything that happens to us can be explained. But we are free not because we have all the answers, but precisely because we don't. The things we cannot explain are the things that teach us we count with God! The mysteries redeem us.

Conclusion

The Governor's Palace in Santa Fe is a building I love to visit. For all its antiquity it is not an ancient building. Made of brown adobe, it is not really an impressive structure. But it was the territorial capital of New Mexico and as such was the governor's "palace" in the territory of New Mexico.

Lew Wallace was once governor of this territory and therefore made his home at the palace. He had long wrangled with the illogical life of Christ. He therefore set about a critical study to examine the miracles and to write a refutation of Jesus, whom he believed was a great historical myth and not the Son of God.

How odd that this Southwestern adobe citadel I love so much should have been the arena of Wallace's early skepticism and later doubt. Within those walls he wrangled on and on over who Jesus was. And the more he studied Christ, the more he became convinced that Christ *was* the Son of God. And so he was inspired to write his famous novel, *Ben Hur*. Who can ever forget the rousing passage in which Ben Hur witnesses the healing of his leprous mother and sister.

Fiction?

Yes.

But from where did the fiction rise? Out of the notion that God works in miraculous ways His wonders to perform. Wake up to doubt and your God will be locked in heaven and you will be jailed on earth. But wake to faith, and miracles will thrust themselves each moment into your awareness. God will become for you the God of infinite possibilities.

It is perhaps worthy of note that when Wallace the Agnostic really encountered the Christ, it was the Christ of Miracles and not the Christ of Philosophical Argument. This should not surprise us. The Christ of miracles is the only Christ there is.

CHAPTER TWO

Miracles: Why Jesus Did Them

Some miracles are so private and sacred that they are not meant to be shared but to be savored quietly in moments of reflection and prayer.

JAMIE MILLER, LAURA LEWIS, JENNIFER SANDER

Whoever else he may have been, Jesus was a miracle worker. All of His claims to be the Son of God were dependent on His miracles. Is this true only of Jesus? Do not Buddhists and Moslems also see their founders in much the same way? Buddhists claim that Gautama walked on water and Moslems claim Mohammud once ascended from the Dome of the Rock. Yet neither of these faith founders is diminished if you take away their miracles. Not so with Christ. Jesus and His miracles come as a single piece. His miracles authenticate His claim and His claims are an inseparable part of His miraculous life. You cannot subtract Christ's miracles and find anything left of Him after the subtraction. If you are to believe in Christ at all it is the miracle-working Jesus you must accept. There is no other Jesus.

Jesus often healed because He was moved by instant compassion. He didn't loiter around the sick to empathize with their suffering. I have a good friend who credits Jesus with his healing from cancer. But he insists his healing began on the day that he told me of his "terminal" illness over the phone. I was overcome with grief at his confession. I asked if I might pray for him over the phone as we talked. He agreed to that and I began to pray. I was aware that my prayer was charged with a great deal of emotion. At times, my voice was so choked I couldn't go on. Even on the phone I could feel my friend's own emotional state as well. At times I could hear him muffling his weeping. When the prayer ended we both gradually returned to the world at hand. We said good-bye and hung up.

Since that long-ago day he says his cancer has been in remission. It has taken me years to feel comfortable talking about it, for the last thing I want to be known as is a healer. I want none of the megalomania sometimes attached to people who claim too much for their prowess as miracle workers. I want to be like Anthony of the Desert preferring complete anonymity in all such matters. Still for years now my friend has continued to minister and is counting on the goodness of God to keep him busy serving Christ in complete health until he must reckon with that finality from which no miracle will spare him.

But there is a further aspect to his deliverance from cancer. Somehow it seems that for one moment in his healing we both took up the ministry of Jesus. And therefore we could understand explicitly that Jesus did care about health and He acted out of compassion to give everyone a better physiology whenever He could. Jesus is seen as the man who righted great wrongs with great wonders. Whenever anyone was in desperate straits, Jesus met their desperation with a quantum of power. In fact, His miracles still furnish the West with metaphors. From Christ's miracles arise such contemporary proverbs as "He's so arrogant he thinks he could walk on water" or "It's your classic case of loaves and fishes" or "Rise, take up your bed and walk" or "Physician, heal thyself!"

Jesus and miracles are nearly synonyms. If there is anything good to be said of contemporary "wonder workers" (of the television genre), it must be said they usually give Jesus all the credit for their miracles. It is sometimes hard to tell if Jesus really wants the credit, but they give it to Him nonetheless. But Jesus' own miracles seem to be a lot less show biz-y and a lot more compassionate than those of contemporary evangelists.

Jesus' miracles are of many different types. For instance, there are the nature miracles, which include the miracles of physical healing. These wonders also demonstrate Jesus' victory over disease—those threats to life which either truncate the length of our days or diminish the quality of our lives. Jesus' nature miracles also include categories of natural wonder, like the stilling of the storm or walking on the water. They repeatedly show the sovereignty of God over all the phenomena of the natural realm.

There is also a group of miracles that deal with sociological compassion. Miracles in this category teach us Jesus' power over the needy field of human relationships. Such miracles include the feeding of the thousands, the creation of wine from water at a wedding, finding the temple tax in a fish's mouth, etc.

The exorcisms of Christ are a final category of miracles. In a way these are among the most important of all His wonders since they illustrate Jesus' final victory over Satan.

I must say, though, that the greatest miracle of all is that in Christ, God became a human being. This is the Grand Miracle: the Incarnation. This most splendid of all the miracles includes within its scope the Virgin Birth, the Resurrection, and the

Ascension. To this miracle we dedicate the *next* chapter of this book. But for the moment let us examine Jesus' miracles in an attempt to find out what they mean for us today.

Looking at the How, What, When, and Why of Jesus' Miracles

The miracles of Jesus number thirty-five. These thirty-five fall into four categories. Nine times Jesus countermanded the natural world. For instance, he turned the water into wine (John 2:1–11), stilled the storm (Matthew 8:23–27) and fed the multitude (Matthew 14:13–21). Six of his recorded miracles were exorcisms (e.g., Mark 1:21–28, Matthew 12:22, Luke 8:26–39). Three times he raised the dead (e.g., Matthew 9:18–26, Luke 7:11–15, John 11:1–44). But the bulk of his miraculous acts were devoted to alleviating suffering. Seventeen times he healed, which earned him the title of Great Physician. Let us therefore focus on miracles of healing because they address our most common need.

So often our need for miracles seems to be less interested in Christ the Healer than the Christ who merely shows up for an "earthly" appearance. Shrines have often been built where Jesus or His mother put in such appearances. The Chapel of the *Quo Vadis* in Rome is one such shrine.

In this tiny little chapel along the Appian Way I once stopped—as do many tourists and pilgrims—to see the footprints of Jesus emblazoned in plaster. Here, according to tradition, Simon Peter met Jesus during the persecutions of Nero.

Peter, under counsel of the persecuted church, was fleeing the city so he would not be captured and martyred. Many in the early church had asked him to leave the city to protect his own life so he could continue to direct the church during those dark days of persecution.

But on his way out of Rome Peter met Jesus, who was going into the city. Peter asked him, "*Quo Vadis, Domine?*" or "Where are you going, Lord?" Jesus told Peter that He was going into the city to be martyred all over again if Peter left it. Whereupon, Peter turned back into Rome and was himself ultimately martyred. The instance became the basis of Sienkiewicz's epic novel *Quo Vadis*.

There is a certain "wow!" effect to all such appearances, but in few cases is anybody really helped by them. There are many "wow!" miracles that take their origin from the last week of Christ's earthly life. One of these reputed miracles may have occurred when St. Veronica loaned Christ her veil as he struggled up Calvary. When He wiped His face with her veil, the imprint of His face came off onto the cloth. This veil has been exhibited across the centuries to extend the "wow" of this miracle to later ages. The Shroud of Turin performed a similar function to believers in our own day.

But evangelicals are not so interested in the appearances of Jesus as in the meaning of the more compassionate miracles He performed. There is little point in Jesus showing up just to say, "Ta-da! Now that I have appeared, build me a shrine!" Miracles should have more meaning, more significance to the church.

Of all the miracles that have meaning, the healing miracles stand front and center for most evangelicals. Why? Pain is a prison. Pain seems to be the enemy of all communion, both human and divine. It fetters the soul to itself. It shuts the soul away in a cask of utter self-concern. As pain grows, we withdraw into a bubble of isolation and wait for the fiery screaming of our nervous systems to pass. When pain is severe enough, we may actually pray to die.

Maria Wilkins was a woman full of bounce, a lover of people, enraptured by the conversation she could not only manage but stimulate. Enter pain and carcinoma. Enter isolation. The last time I saw her, she was wailing in agony in ward thirty-two, a dehumanized, sallow-eyed, and sunken-cheeked replica of life. She and her cancer died that same afternoon. At the moment of her passing, she abandoned life without even speaking to her friends. Indeed, she did not even want them present.

I was her pastor, but I counted her also a friend (as I do all members of my church). I had prayed often—in her presence—for her pain to end. As I watched her die, I had the oddest feeling my prayer was answered. Why? Her pain did end. To be sure, I personally would have liked her to leave her hospital existence and move back into her once-healthy earthly life. But the key thing is that Jesus met the pain and took it away even as he took her across the threshold of immortality.

Remember what we've already established: Heaven is the finest and most final of Christian miracles. There, pain is not permitted. Maria had found that beyond the morphine was Revelation 21:4: "He will wipe every tear from their eyes. There will be no more death or mourning or crying or pain, for the old order of things has passed away."

So my prayers were, in a sense, effective. She has been healed, never again to deal with pain.

It is an amazing thing. A miracle of healing sends the power of God into that strange inner world of 98.6-degree darkness. There, beneath the surface of our personalities, lies a strange cosmos of gristle and pulsating tendons, of ventricles and spongy glands, of rubbery pipes and cartilage. When a miraculous healing occurs, God enters this soft and unseen world; the amino acids then stand to attention, nuclei bow in preparation for the coming storm of renovation, and God's miracle visits the dark warm world of biology.

Disease always cringed before the healing miracles of Christ. Consider the woman with the incessant hemorrhage (Luke 8:43–48). When she first contracted the condition, Jesus was still a teenager. She grew old hoping for a cure, coping with life. She craved wholeness. She spent all she had searching for health. Finally, she heard of Jesus. She came to Him. She touched his garment and instantly was healed. We do not know what caused her bleeding, but let us say it was leukemia. This is a poor guess, but if it were leukemia, let us observe what happened. Upon touching Jesus's robe, the quarreling corpuscles in her arteries and veins ceased their disputes. The white cells gave up their ghastly civil struggle with their red brothers. Instantly the cellular cannibalism ended, and she was well.

Perhaps you object that such a description of the miracle is too clinical. But let us remember that if the poor woman was to be free of leukemia, the deadly battle of her blood cells had to be reversed. If we cannot believe this happened, we cannot believe this miracle.

Jesus' healing miracles rebukes nature, which God created as good, for becoming malevolent. His nature miracles do, too. Jesus once rebuked a storm. He spoke to the wind—moving molecules of hydrogen, oxygen, carbon dioxide, and nitrogen. He rebuked the storm, and at His rebuke the wind subsided. But how did Christ communicate with the moving molecules? They have no auditory nerves to hear. They are merely kinetic functions. Still, at His rebuke the molecules did in some way yield. The wild atmosphere was tamed.

When I was a boy in Enid, Oklahoma, a faith healer came to our small town and created a stir of controversy with his crusades. He claimed to heal some sick people, but after he left, they returned to their previous state of illness. However, in time he became one of the popular faith healers of our day. The reaction of our hometown to the healer was much like the reaction of Nazarenes to Jesus. Some said of the healer that his failure to heal people permanently was because Enid was not the epicenter of biblical faith. As it was said of Nazareth so it was said of Enid: Christ could "do no mighty works there . . . And he marveled because of their unbelief" (Mark 6:5–6). Of course, many others just thought the healer was a fraud.

But are all faith healers inept or dishonest? I don't think so. Michael Arvey writes that George Orr lost the sight in his right eye. This happened in 1925 when George worked at the Lawrence Foundry Company in Grove City, Pennsylvania. Apparently, while he was working one day at an open cauldron, a fleck of molten iron flew up into his eye, taking his sight. A scar soon formed over the cornea. George's doctor, Dr. C. E. Imbrie, said that Orr would always be blind in that eye and nothing could be done about it.

But on May 4, 1971, Orr attended a Kathryn Kuhlman healing service and prayed for healing. Arvey wrote, "Suddenly his eye began to tingle and flow with tears. Driving home, Orr realized he could see out of his right eye. The scar had vanished. The cure was instantaneous, complete, and permanent."[6]

I have freely confessed in this book that I had a parish member that once went to a faith healer and was cured of his blindness. It wasn't the fact that he was cured that bothered me, it was the fact that I didn't really want it to happen the way it did that bothered me. I didn't much care for the methods of the "wonder worker" he chose to perform his miracle. He seemed to me (and to most of my friends) to be a rabbit-in-the-hat kind of a faith healer whose show-biz methods turned me off. I think I would really have preferred him go to Lourdes. I don't have a great deal of confidence in Lourdes as a sure-fire place of miracles either, but somehow it seems a better bet than the glitzy, jet-setting scoundrel my friend chose. Still, the late Kathryn Kuhlman was—as are many contemporary healers—always eager to give God the full credit for all the healings she secured. Once more Michael Arvey tells of another method that Kuhlman used in her crusades. As was customary, Kuhlman told her crowd, "I'm a nobody. I have no power. But the Holy Spirit heals. I am only his instrument." Then, after a few moments of silence, she said, "The Holy Spirit is healing someone right now. It's a woman . . . down here on the ground floor . . . She had a cancer . . . of the lungs. And now . . . She is being healed. You know who you are. Stand up and come forward to claim your healing." To the amazement of the crowd a woman left her seat and came upon the stage to confess her healing.

Following that incident Kuhlman continued to point to different areas of the audience, calling for more healings. "There's a woman with a bronchial condition in the chorus. That bronchial condition is now gone. There's a man down front with a heart condition. I rebuke that heart condition. There's a child with diabetes. The sugar is gone from his body. There's someone in the audience who has a tumor . . . They are supposed to have an operation in a week. But God wants you to know the tumor is gone."[7]

According to Avery, Dr. Nolen, a skeptical physician, investigated several people who claimed they had been healed by Kuhlman. In the end he said his search for even one authentic miracle had never been realized.

But I am not so skeptical myself. Am I more prone to believe because I have more confidence in the healer than Dr. Nolen?

No. For as I have already confessed, I have very little confidence in showy faith healers. But I do hold a great deal of confidence in the power of faith exhibited by the suffering. Those who live with pain in many cases reach out in needy ways to the Great Physician and are healed. It is the faith of the sufferer that heals and not the healer.

How often in Scripture does Jesus say, "Your faith has saved you" or "Your faith has made you whole"? Jesus gives great power to those who hold the faith! "If you have faith as great as a grain of mustard seed, you can say to this mountain, be moved and cast into the depth of the sea" (Matthew 17:20). The miracle of mountain moving is always faith reliant.

Could those whose faith heals them in the presence of a faith healer find healing without going to a faith healer? Yes, of course. Still, their faith seems to gain a bit more ardor when they are in front of a wonder worker or are actually touched by one.

Oral Roberts himself, who suffered from a terrible killing affliction in adolescence, was touched and healed by such a wonder worker. The powerful effect of such a "touch and be cured" process never left him. This was the very sort of ministry he extended to others throughout his ministry. How many times in my own ministry have I gathered with members of our church ministry team and laid hands on the sick and prayed for their healing? Did they get well? Some of them. Did they die? Some of them. In the case of those who did not die, did my seeming nonmiracle stop me from asking God to heal others later?

Of course not!

I continued my praying, healing ministry for three reasons. First, it is always right to ask God for what we want. If we want to see a friend feel better, we must tell Jesus. God's will must always be served and we must accept it when we don't get what we want. But God is our Father. As any earthly father wants his children to ask for the desires of their hearts, so does God. What earthly father would want his children to cower in doubt, never asking because they had no confidence?

Second, it is always better to intercede for someone else than it is to ask them to pray for themselves. Intercession is most powerful not when we pray for our own needs, but when others pray for us, for in such cases we bypass all self-serving prayers. Mother Teresa of Calcutta forbad her sisters of Charity to pray for their own illnesses. They could enlist the prayers of others for their needs, but they could not pray for themselves.

Third, my ministry of prayer for other people's healing does include touch. In our current politically correct world, we're afraid to touch. We have a great fear of "violating someone else's space." To touch crosses that boundary. Why do it? Because all of us have a screaming need to be touched. Touch is the last dare of political correctness. Touch is going as far as we can to assure someone else that we are really there with them. If we refuse to touch, we cannot offer this last, best certification of human nearness.

When we touch as we talk to God, a new kind of prayer power is born. The speech is to Jesus, but the feel of skin-to-skin nearness welcomes the final certification of miracle. It can happen! I've been in the presence of real faith as human trust reaches out to God. Then my own flagging faith has been given the last bit of leap it needs to believe. I can be healed. I am healed. Be quiet, you clamoring pain. Die, you bacteria! Retreat, gangrene! You must give up your hold on me! I have been touched by a God-lover. He has called in help from his friend Jesus. Now get yourself ready for the coming storm of power. Now I am free of disease.

In your heart you may argue, "Is it that easy? Does it always work like *this*?" No. But it always works. Sometimes touch and prayer makes the sickness go away. Sometimes it merely helps the suffering bear their sickness. Often it is simply those standing by the sufferer who are comforted. But it always works and therefore it is always right to pray and touch.

Dr. William Nolen, the skeptical physician I referred to above, spent much time investigating and trying to corroborate Kuhlman's ministry. His conclusions were not in her favor. Dr. Nolen suggested this kind of evaluation: Imagine yourself at a Kuhlman crusade. You are suffering from a hurting back. Kathryn Kuhlman says, "All you with a bad back, stand up. Go into the aisles." You obey her and go into the aisle. Now you are aware that thousands of people are watching, so when Kathryn Kuhlman says "Bend," are you going to stand there, rigid, like some sort of ninny? You are going to bend . . . even if it kills you. Nolen suggests a kind of spell takes charge of the audience. There are wheelchairs on the stage, and lines forming to claim cures. It all seems most hypnotic. But "The spell is not real," Nolen asserted. "None of the patients [I] examined had been miraculously cured of anything, by either Kathryn Kuhlman or the Holy Spirit."[8]

Most thinking people are skeptical of these antics Dr. Nolen describes. Yet even in the midst of such glitzy healing, we must leave some place for an authentic miracle to occur. Remember: of the thousands of miracles reported at Lourdes, only sixty-six have been certified. Surely these same kinds of odds must hold for the healing work of televangelists.

Generally most of us have the impression that Jesus was far more authentic and that all of His miracles could be certified. Faith was what the needy gave to Jesus and healing is what He returned to them. Faith is important for healing. Let us ask three questions concerning Christ's healing miracles: How did Christ heal? When did He do it? Why did He heal?

How Did Christ Heal?

How? Sometimes He used saliva, sometimes touch. Sometimes He embraced the sufferer. Sometimes He spoke to the disease. Sometimes He forgave sin, and the cure came with His forgiveness. When we look at how Jesus healed, the one word from Scripture that strikes us is the word *immediately*. Twenty-three times in the New Testament the word *immediately* is used to tell how Jesus healed or performed miracles. In every one of the seventeen recorded healing miracles, it was instantly clear to those at hand that the suffering one had been healed.

I once saw a faith healer with a most unusual approach. He would stand before a large crowd and say, "There is a man in this audience who is on row thirty, and he has been suffering for years from kidney infections. Sir, God wants you to know that you have been miraculously healed! Stand and give God the glory!" And then, in a kind of response to the healer's clairvoyance, a man would stand in what appeared to be row thirty and give God the glory. And in a similarly clairvoyant method, patients with heart disease, ulcers, colitis, rheumatism, and so on were cured row by row, section by section. But these cures were not immediately visible to those around them in the stands.

I was skeptical, because I remembered a family who called me after a faith-healing service to tell me that their diabetic daughter had been miraculously cured and would never again need insulin. "The Lord has miraculously healed her," they said. They confidently reported that they had the word of their favorite media evangelist who had performed this great miracle. Their daughter had been touched by this charismatic healer. The Spirit had been called down. Glory be to God! She was cured!

I rejoiced with them, but reminded them that they should watch for early signs of insulin shock. They countered my suggestion by saying that even to look for signs of the disease after she had been certified "healed" would be to exhibit weak faith. To demonstrate the hardiness (maybe the foolhardiness) of their faith, they threw away their store of insulin and syringes. A week later they called me in the small hours of the morning to report that their daughter was in a deep coma and could not be roused. I urged them to take her to the emergency room of the nearest hospital. Only a physician's skill was able to deliver their daughter from the "miracle" of the faith healer.

In marked contrast, Jesus' miracles were both instantaneous and apparent. He gave false hopes to none. How did He heal? He did so *without* personal gratuities or love offerings, and usually *with* immediate physical evidence.

In the early years of the twentieth century one of America's great faith healers was dying. Before she did she confessed that she had amassed a fortune through her crusades. At the time of her death, she had jewels and antiques worth over a million dollars, purchased from the love offerings of her devotees. How differently Jesus offered his healing. There was no hint of selfishness or personal gain in Jesus' ministry among the poor of Palestine. Every disciple should glory in following a Christ who died in poverty.

When Did Christ Heal?

When did Jesus heal? Whenever people asked for it. In cases of demoniacs or the dumb who could not ask, Jesus set them free anyway (Matthew 9:32, 12:22, 17:14). The great concern of those who brought their mute friends to Christ stirred Him to touch and heal those who could not ask for their own healing.

As we said earlier of miracles in general, Christ usually healed in response to human desperation. Catherine Marshall in *A Man Called Peter* tells how she was healed during a broadcast as her husband Peter Marshall preached a radio sermon on the healing power of Christ. Likewise, the wife of a good pastor friend of mine was hopelessly stricken with cancer. During exploratory surgery it was diagnosed as "terminal within a few weeks." She sensed her own desperation and yielded in total obedience to Christ's will, and she was granted healing. Every time I see her now, years later, I am reminded what God can do with desperation.

The simple answer to "When does Christ heal?" should always be "At the moment when someone who is hurting and needy asks for it." Of all the miracles of Lourdes, I am prone to believe all of the sixty-six miracles that have been certified. When did they happen? When faith met need.

On December 17, 1899, an express train on the Bordeaux-Paris line rear-ended another train stopped in the station of Augoulème. Gabriel Gargam, the guard, was hurled into the snow twenty-five yards away from his pulverized mail wagon. It was hours later before he was found. He was in a coma. The doctors could confirm neither a fracture nor a break in his spinal column, but it was easy to see that he was paralyzed. His collarbone was broken, and his body was covered with cuts.

Though he finally came out of the coma, Gargam lay in the hospital for months, artificially fed because he was unable to swallow. He dwindled to a skeleton and had no feeling in his body. He was discharged from his job in August 1901. He received workman's disability compensation of sixty thousand francs along with an annual pension from the French railways.

Under pressure from his family, especially his mother, Gargam reluctantly agreed to be taken to Lourdes. There he was immersed in Lourdes water on August 20, 1901. He fainted. During the afternoon sacramental procession he suddenly got up from his stretcher, tottered laboriously around, and asked for something to eat. Within three months he had put on twenty-two pounds. His cure was permanent.[9]

However, a Catholic friend of mine went to Lourdes to seek healing. She did not receive healing and came back still suffering from the malady that took her there. Even in the face of desperate need, some are not healed. We have to trust that God has His purpose.

Let us not forget that salvation always comes when the lost are made aware of their utter helplessness. Why should the same thing not be true in physiology? If God can cure desperate souls, why not desperate bodies? The woman of Luke 8 was cured partly because she had tried everything else to no avail. Bartimaeus of Jericho cried out, soul-weary with years of blindness. Those near him rebuked him and told him to be silent. He refused. He wanted to see—he was desperate to behold the light of day. And he did.

There are times when Jesus asked a blind man—perhaps a beggar—"What wilt thou have me do?" The answer was obvious, and yet he asked. He wanted the one in need to deal with his own priorities. Did the beggar really want to be well? Hypochondria is a formidable barrier to health. Unlike Bartimaeus, hypochondriacs have no real need to be healthy—only a furious hunger to be pitied.

For years a member of my church was a hypochondriac. On pastoral calls, I often stopped by her home. Whenever she served me tea, the tea cart would be crowded with medicines. Often, as I observed her taking two or three pills during a single cup of tea, an overwhelming sense of anger arose within me. Like Christ in the Temple, I wanted to turn over the trays of drugs and drive out the demons of hypochondria that filled her with self-pity. This woman never asked me to pray for her to get well. She reveled in her supposed illnesses.

Jesus on the other hand usually healed when those who asked demonstrated a genuine feeling of desperation. At the point of ultimate need, physiology and spirituality have the most in common. Repentance is not a drab recounting of error. Repentance is utter desperation: engulfed in our own sin, we are utterly overwhelmed at our powerlessness to rise above it. Repentance is facing the fact that our sins resulted in the cross. We cry to God, "Lord, have mercy on me, a sinner."

Likewise, Jesus heals physically when we cry, "Lord, have mercy!" There are times when the despair of suffering drives us to the wall of consciousness. Antibiotics and chemotherapy have all failed, and the specialists say, "I'm sorry, there's nothing more we can do." The gallant Christ then looms in compassion above our need.

Why Did Christ Heal?

Why did Christ heal? Because pain is a prison! Mark 1:29–31 (KJV) says:

> *And forthwith, when they were come out of the synagogue, they entered into the house of Simon and Andrew, with James and John. But Simon's wife's mother lay sick of a fever. He came and took her by the hand, and lifted her up; and immediately the fever left her, and she ministered unto them.*

Christ heals those who ask for help. It might be for physical help, such as for Simon's mother-in-law. It might even be for mental pain and anguish. I read recently of something that happened to Janice Stiehler of Baldwin, New York. She said she "worried on the night of the Yankees game her teenage son was attending, for the game had gone into extra innings." She knew that Kurt and his friends would have to take the Penn Station subway. This would have to be done in the wee small hours of the morning. She went to sleep but woke at precisely 1:10 A.M. when she heard the crash of a shattered windowpane. At first she thought someone was breaking into her house. Frightened, she woke her husband and both of them searched the house but found no evidence of burglars or of broken glass. But her son Kurt was still not home.

"For some reason, I felt compelled to pray for him," Janice remembers. So she sat down in the kitchen, prayed—and waited. "An hour later, a Penn Station security officer phoned. The boys had been horsing around at the terminal, and Kurt's arm had crashed through a huge storefront window. The broken glass pieces were so jagged and heavy that the arm should have been completely severed. But Kurt had sustained no injury, not even a scratch.

"When did this happen?" Janice asked.

"About one-fifteen," came the answer.

Then Janice understood. She had been awakened just in time to pray for Kurt. And somehow, across the miles, her prayers had protected him.[10]

The passage from Mark also makes it clear that sickness gets in the way of serving others—perhaps another reason Jesus chose to heal so many. It is not so noteworthy that Simon's mother-in-law was healed. It is noteworthy that on being healed, she immediately got out of bed and began serving the people at her house. Miracles bear within them the obligation of service. God has an infinite supply of power, but once He heals us, we are responsible to use our new health to serve Him and others.

After Jesus cast the demons out of Mary, she anointed Him with spikenard. After Jesus cast the horde of demons out of Legion, He commissioned the healed man to be an apostle to the people of his own country. After Jesus miraculously confronted Saul on the Damascus road, Paul became an apostle to the Gentiles. So many times miracles are followed by a clear mandate to serve. Perhaps the first question that should come to the healed is "Now that I have health, how am I to spend it . . . and on what?"

Perhaps the most dramatic evidence of this occurred at the Sea of Galilee during Jesus' third resurrection appearance to his disciples. When the disciples arrived at the shore, Jesus had already built a fire. Jesus' greatest miracle—the miracle of the Resurrection—was followed by Christ's own humble act of service in which He builds a campfire.

So, referring again to the question, "Why does Christ heal?" there is one simple answer: to set us free. The greatest miracle we receive is the new birth. Jesus assumes that after we receive this great miracle, we will be eager, like Simon's healed mother-in-law, to rise and begin to serve our world. While the new birth will likely bring us greater joy than our service does, both of them are only stops along a never-ending continuum of service and praise. Many people who claim they have been "saved" are never caught serving their Lord. What a wasted and lamentable end for a miracle.

Why did Christ focus so much on healing when He came primarily to redeem? I don't believe He worked His miracles to confirm His Messiah-ship. Yet neither were they incidental to His greater purpose. The answer must lie in His godhood. He healed primarily because He was a Christ of love.

Five times prior to a miracle the Scriptures say, "He was moved with compassion." Eight times prior to a miracle, "He had compassion on them." Perhaps the why of Christ's healing should not be so puzzling. Would you expect the Messiah to walk by a crippled child and say, "Poor thing! I could help you run in the sunlight in complete health, but what good would it do? You would only grow old in fifty years and die anyway. And after all, I am on a mission of salvation. Believe you me, little girl, temporal suffering is just nothing compared to what awaits you"? A Christ who was *that* busy with saving the world would not be loving enough to redeem it.

Still, He was not *primarily* the Great Physician but the savior of the world. Had He been only a healer, He could have stood on Olivet and rebuked all suffering at once. But He came to earth to die. And the same love that brought Him here to die caused Him to heal while He awaited His cross. In anticipation of the iron ripping through His own wrists, He could not be flippant about the pain He saw destroying others.

Jesus also performed miracles to deal with other kinds of suffering. The fear of His apostles, when they were caught in a violent storm, made Him walk to them on the sea. His compassion for the hungry among the peasants persuaded Him to divide the loaves. His compassion for the embarrassed wedding host prompted Him to turn water into wine.

Relieving discomfort, however, was not His only aim. As I said earlier, suffering destroys all interest in other values, either social or spiritual. So by restoring health, Christ made a way for those who were in pain to find release from their prison of self-concern.

Conclusion

One final suggestion may be made as to why Jesus healed. He viewed the human body as a temple. Jesus' indictment as a false Messiah arose from outrage at His statement, "Destroy this temple and I will raise it again in three days" (John 2:19 NIV). The body was the temple. A healthy temple is a better center of worship than a diseased one (see Matthew 23:27). Concern for health is a wholesome witness to a God who created us whole. The body is to glorify God (see 1 Corinthians 6:16–20) and be glorified by God (see 1 Corinthians 15:51–57). Every fleshly temple will be whole in eternity. Heaven will be free from all disease and suffering. Perhaps the healing miracles of Christ are his way of bearing witness to the final glory we will receive.

Someday in that new world his church will sit down in the councils of heaven. Those who died of plague, leukemia, polio and, as Hamlet said, "the thousand natural shocks that flesh is heir to" will be there. Then they will not remember the awful pain that closed their window of earthly existence. Nor will they remember the long-ago world of bacteria, infection, and death. Millions of believers will glorify God in bodies that will never again experience a headache or a bruise. Then the only scars left in the entire universe will be the stigmata of Christ which the Father will leave in his hands so that we will remember how much he loves us.[11]

CHAPTER THREE

The Virgin Birth Miracle: How God Came to Planet Earth

*In the Christian story God descends to reascend. He comes down;
down from the heights of absolute being into time and space,
down into humanity; down further still, if embryologists are right,
to recapitulate in the womb ancient and pre-human phases of life;
down to the very roots and seabed of the Nature He has created.*

C. S. LEWIS

God becoming a man in Christ is made possible by the two miracles that serve as bookends to Jesus' thirty-three years of earthly life. The first of these miracles is the Virgin Birth which brought Jesus into the human condition. The second is the Resurrection-Ascension, which took Him out of it. These two miracles are the pillars on which rests the doctrine that in Christ, God became a man. I need those two miracles because I have two needs for God. I need Him to be human so He can understand me and I need Him to be more than human so He can help me. But of these two miracles, it is the miracle of the Virgin Birth that has been so hotly contested by the liberal scholars of the nineteenth and twentieth centuries. These thinkers usually downplay the significance of the Virgin birth by saying that to be fully human (as we all insist Jesus must be), Jesus must have been born in a fully human way and therefore have had a fully human father. They argued that if Jesus really had no human father, as Scripture attests, could he really be fully human?

The chief fallacy of such an argument is that the Bible teaches that Christ was conceived without an earthly father (Luke 1:34–35). If we permit ourselves to agree that the Bible falsifies this, how can we ever be sure that the rest of the life of Christ, with all its attendant miracles, has been properly reported?

Marcion, a second-century scholar, rewrote the early Gospel of Luke, expunging all these portions of the text he disagreed with, and wound up with only a hit-and-miss Jesus whose miracles were so depleted, it became impossible to tell which stories about Him were true and which were not. This early heretic accepted Christ the teacher but not Christ the miracle worker.

I have a scholar friend who says he rejects the Virgin Birth because it is non-essential to believe it to be "saved." His argument is that when he came to faith at a young age, he didn't even know "what a virgin was." Since God saved him without this understanding, the Virgin Birth had no real part to play in his redemption.

I reminded him that even though he was "saved" without understanding the Virgin Birth, had he grown to maturity and then had to ask, "Does the Bible tell the truth about this?" His mature faith would collapse. Why? Because of the inconsistency of trying to hold on to what he earlier believed about Christ when later evidence contradicted it. Even as children, we find our early teachings must coincide with our mature understanding of faith or we will never continue believing in Christ.

It is much like believing in "the doctrine of Santa Claus." I ardently believed this doctrine at age four, but at fourteen I found I had to dismiss that belief because I could no longer hold it with any credibility. The stack of yuletide facts did not support the doctrine. But the facts at every later step of maturity do go on supporting the doctrine of the Virgin Birth.

The Virgin Birth may not be dismissed without setting our faith in the entire New Testament at risk. Upon this doctrine hangs the issue of Jesus' entrance into time. To call it a lie is to say that the church must be willing to opt for "adoptionism." Adoptionism is the belief that Jesus was not always God's son. The view teaches that Christ was merely a human being born naturally as the son of Mary and Joseph. Adoptionists see Jesus as a human being of such triumphant morality and wisdom that when He became a mature adult God proudly adopted Him.

I am God's child by adoption (see Romans 8) and this makes me the brother of Christ. But I am ill at ease in saying that both Jesus and I got to be sons the same way. He was God's Son "in essence" from eternity past. I only became God's son in 1945 when he adopted me because of my confession. I treasure my sonship, but it is vastly different from Christ's.

Adoption is a Unitarian concept of how Jesus "came to be" God's Son. To accept the view is to argue that Jesus never made his entrance into human flesh in exactly the way Matthew and Luke say he did. Adoptionism is then the only alternative—nonbiblical though it be—to explain how Jesus came to be God's Son.

There is no miracle in the idea of Christ's being adopted. But it is a huge miracle when we are. John Newton called it his miracle of *amazing grace*. What happened to him when he was supernaturally, miraculously born? He said he came to sight, having once been blind. He had once been lost but considered himself found. Though he once was mortal he would live for ten thousand years.

So to be born again endows us with the same eternal attributes Jesus acquired in his Virgin Birth.

The birth narratives of Matthew and Luke spin us into a world of high miracle and even higher spirituality. God became a man. He stooped to conquer. He descended into greatness. He did all this by setting aside normal genetics and stepping around the ordered world of genes and chromosomes to become the Incarnate Son of God. Yes, the angels sang, the shepherds adored, and the wise men came from afar. But more than the more sentimental aspects of the story, God became a real man in Christ.

We dare not separate the truth of such miracles from the integrity of what the Bible teaches about them. Either the Virgin Birth happened the way Luke said it did, or the rest of Luke (and Matthew too) may not be depended on. We cannot have a Bible that is true in some places but not in others. Liberal theologians once charged that the Virgin Birth was invented by early Christians who saw normal conception and birth as a "slur on sexuality." But C. S. Lewis once remarked the Virgin Birth was no more a slur on sex than the feeding of the five thousand was a slur on the bakeries of the day.

Jesus, Son of Mary, Son of God

In 1208 Mary is said to have delivered the Rosary to St. Dominic. Not only was the Rosary to achieve spiritual significance in the Church, but through it Mary herself rose to new levels of prominence.[12] Mary is not as prominent in Scripture as she has become in the centuries of tradition that have occurred since. Nonetheless, the importance given to her by the church does find their roots in the Bible.

But what do the Scriptures teach about her? She was called to be the *theotokos* –the "god bearer." She was a virgin when she received her calling and many Christians believe that she remained a virgin for the rest of her life. But her perpetual virginity is a moot point with Protestants and other evangelicals. Evangelicals take the position that she was the *theotokos* but not a perpetual virgin. They believe that other children were born to her and Joseph after Jesus was born. The "children of Mary" mentioned in Mark 6:3–4 are to be seen as her "naturally born" children.

This is my view. It does not dampen my esteem for either Mary or the role she played in bringing Jesus to the human race. To me Mary's exaltation derives from three things: her obedience to God, her human suffering, and her steadfastness in sticking with Jesus all the way to the cross. I lift her in high admiration . . . but I offer her no adoration. Why?

First, I honor her for her obedience to God. In Luke 1:30, Gabriel tells Mary she has "found favor." Mary by her life of obedience to God, won the smile of God, and he selected her to be the God bearer.

Second, I honor Mary for her suffering. When the infant Jesus was presented at the temple (for his circumcision, no doubt), Simeon, the old Patriarch who blessed the baby said to Mary, "A sword will pierce through your own soul" (Luke 2:35 NKJV). The word here for *sword* is the word *romphaia*, meaning a steel Persian sword long enough to skewer the small body of this Nazarene mother.

Simeon's prophecy came true when Mary was forced to watch her beloved Jesus die on the cross. Her suffering was immense. (But while Mary's suffering was great, she herself plays no significant role in human redemption. Christ alone provides our salvation with his suffering.)

My third reason for affirming Mary comes because Mary stuck with Jesus all the way to the cross. This makes the son and his mother appear a team in the single plan of God. Some theologians believe Revelation 12 speaks of this great redemptive team of Mary and Jesus.

> *A great and wondrous sign appeared in heaven: a woman clothed with the sun, with the moon under her feet and a crown of twelve stars on her head. She was pregnant and cried out in pain as she was about to give birth. Then another sign appeared in heaven: an enormous red dragon with seven heads and ten horns and seven crowns on his head. His tail swept a third of the stars out of the sky and flung them to the earth. The dragon stood in front of the woman who was about to give birth, so that he might devour her child the moment it was born. She gave birth to a son, a male child, who will rule all the nations with an iron scepter. And her child was snatched up to God and to his throne. (Revelation 12:1–5 NIV)*

While most evangelicals believe the woman in the passage speaks of the nation Israel, some insist the passage is a confirmation of Mary's role in human redemption and her subsequent enthronement in the heavens.

Many Christians believe that Mary still "heals" at shrines worldwide, but her most frequent wonders have more to do with her appearances than her miracles. Indeed, her appearances themselves seem to be her miracles, since her first major appearance in 1008 C.E. to a group of churchgoers in Valenciennes, France. Her most recent "certified" appearance was at Medjugorie, Yugoslavia, which is currently called Bosnia, Herzegovina. I have visited the Shrine of Guadalupe in Mexico and been amazed at Mary's continual exultation among the poor of

Mexico. Often crowds of pilgrims can be heard to shout, "Long live Mexico, long live the Virgin!" It strikes me as an odd blend of patriotism and worship. Yet this great shrine and cathedral stands to mark the moment when Juan Diego, a poor Indian, saw Mary in 1534, in the early days of Spanish establishment. On Juan Diego's cloak (revered as the Tilma) is the imprint of the Virgin. While the cactus-cloth cloak ought to have disintegrated by now, it is still said to be in miraculously good condition.

This same curious and romantic regard for Mary is found throughout the American Southwest. My home in New Mexico is not far from the Chimayo shrine where thousands have gone for healing. Not too far from there, in May of 1978, a New Mexico mother, Maria Rubio, was frying tortillas and the hot grease seared the face of Jesus onto one of her tortillas. She has preserved the tortilla under glass and it has for many become an object of worship.[13]

But Mary's miracles and appearances are virtually unknown among evangelicals. The Virgin Birth of Christ accords her no spiritual power for contemporary miracle-working. In spite of her elevation in the Catholic Church few Protestants turn to her for supernatural help. One of the few is the American pilot who fell "behind enemy lines" in the movie that tells his tale. He gave credit to his survival to the Virgin, (perhaps to the Virgin of Medjugorie, which is not too far from the site where this pilot crash-landed).

But one aspect of the Catholic Church's traditional view of the Virgin Birth must be applauded: while many Protestant theologians have doubted the doctrine, the Catholics have not. I have personally met many Protestant scholars who do not believe the Virgin Birth. But I have never met a Catholic cleric who doubts it. We should take our lesson from them. The doctrine that is rooted in Matthew and Luke's Gospels is incontrovertible and must be maintained as a miracle of supreme importance.

The Virgin Birth: The Way of the Incarnation

So Jesus, the virgin-born Son of God must be both divine and human, both God and man. Charles Wesley's Christmas carol invites us to consider:

Veiled in flesh, the Godhead see
Hail the Incarnate Deity.
Born as man, with men to dwell
Jesus our Immanuel... [14]

Unless Jesus is fully man He cannot understand us. Unless He is fully God He cannot help us. He must be both the Son of God and Mary.

It is even as our thumb-worn creeds say it is: while many men have tried to be gods, only once did God ever become a man and thus we are saved by Immanuel, which in Hebrew means "God is with us." And with us He redeems. No wonder Madeline L'Engle once said, "There is only one real miracle—the Incarnation. It alone makes the rest of Jesus' miracles possible."

But what does it mean to say God became a man and only by lowering Himself in this way was he able to save us?

I remember reading years ago that Billy Graham was walking with his son in the North Carolina woods near their home. As they walked along the evangelist stepped on an ant den and crushed to death a great many insects. His young son bent down and watched the ants twitching in the spasms of dying. "Isn't there anything we can do to help them?" he asked.

"No," replied the evangelist. "Only if I could somehow become an ant would I even have the possibility of understanding them. Only then could I help."

In Philippians 2, Paul said that what Jesus did was vast and cosmos-wide: God emptying himself and dwindling down to human size to help the human race by becoming a citizen of the race. No wonder the Father said to the Singer:

Give me your vast infinity My Son;
I'll wrap it in a bit of clay.
Then enter Terra microscopically
To love the little souls who weep away
Their lives. [15]

The Singer agreed to it and said:

And then I fell asleep and all awareness fled.
I felt my very being shrinking down.
My vastness ebbed away. In dwindling dread,
All size decayed. The universe around
Drew back. I woke upon a tiny bed
Of straw in one of Terra's smaller towns. [16]

Thus God became a human being for the sake of human beings. But what we do with Christ is unthinkable. In examining the person of Christ, there exists the tendency either to tilt too far in the direction of His humanity or His godhood. Generally speaking, the novels and movies that depict Him are far more prone to speak of His human nature than His godhood.

Years ago I was offended when in *Jesus Christ Superstar* Mary Magdalene sang to Andrew Lloyd Webber's neurotic Jesus, "Try not to be worried, try not to be harried, try not to turn on the problems that upset you." So human was this stagestruck Messiah, he was marketed worldwide as a fame-seeking rock star. Not a true picture of Christ!

Still, as we indicated earlier, some theologians have supported this odd notion. Nels F. S. Ferré said, "The Virgin Birth separated Jesus from the human race with a kind of radical discontinuity." Emil Brunner also believed that the Virgin Birth did not unite Christ with humanity but separated Him from it. But Brunner went even further in claiming that it left Jesus only half-God and half-man, rather than all God and all man (which is the traditional view).

To hold that Jesus is the Son of God, there are only two courses of reason open to us: The Virgin Birth (a view of Orthodoxy) must be separated from Adoptionism (a non-Trinitarian view). We must either accept the Virgin Birth, by which Jesus exists as the Son of God in supernatural essence, or we must move to some lesser theory. Many scholars—myself included—believe the point at which God adopted Jesus was at His baptism. The *Bath Qol* (Aramaic for "loud voice") cried out over the Jordan River and this moment became the point of God's adoption of Christ.

Why did God get loud when he thundered above the river at Jesus' baptism? With this loud voice God distinctly affirmed His Son. Though I don't want to trivialize the event, I do think looking at the divine pronouncement in very earthly terms may help us. The sequence seems almost like what a human father might do when his son has just achieved some important athletic event. Have you not heard an excited father at some athletic event shout, "Hey! Look out there! That's my boy!"

If putting the event in such earthly terms is too much of a stretch, see God as He reaches out in affirmation toward Jesus. For thirty years Jesus had been coming to a messianic awareness of who He was and what God had called Him to do. This struggle for identity must have dogged His steps. He desired obedience, but He struggled to understand what it meant to be the Son of God.

Into this struggle came God's oral affirmation—the loud voice. God spoke, and in this single utterance all that Jesus had arrived at through personal struggle was proven true. The God of Israel cried: "I am God. This is my beloved son! Look at this paragon of obedience. Look at this sinless victor over all temptation! Look at this God-man, committed to my plan for world redemption. I am pleased!"

The voice above the river also carries an implicit question: Is God's Son God to us? Are we eager to obey Him, knowing that our obedience is as sweet to Him as His obedience was to His Father?

Conclusion

What can the Virgin Birth teach me about living the Christ-life? For each of us Christ should be the great example for living. Just as, through Mary, God took on human flesh and complimented humankind by indwelling us, so I am to take within myself this great God and become a "mini-incarnation" of Christ.

Every birth is a miracle of grace, but, as Augustine once used the term, it is a severe grace. When I was born, like every other child, I had to take a perilous trip down the constricting birth canal and enter the harshness of my environment. Yet birth was where I began life. Perhaps that is why I have joined other evangelicals in protesting abortion. It seems somehow set against my own right to journey into life. Mine is not a particularly noble life, but it is endowed with the right to be. How much more do I respect all truly great lives, from Einstein to Mozart. And, best of all, Jesus, who in His own seven-pound trip down the birth canal somehow certifies every human's right to be born.

For through the Virgin Birth God took upon Himself a "robe of flesh" and entered the human arena with me. He and I meet as fellow human beings who together can enjoy the label *homo-sapiens*.

This miracle offers us a double confidence. That God became a person means He cares for us. That He remains both God and a person means that I can turn to Him for help. Therefore the Incarnation certifies all miracles.

For me, Jesus moved into my world in becoming a man!

The Incarnation is God with my zip code. Christ is God on my block, doing mighty things for me because He is all God and all man. Who would want to serve any other God?

CHAPTER FOUR

The Resurrection: The Queen of Miracles

In their fright the women bowed down with their faces to the ground, but the men said to them, 'Why do you look for the living among the dead? He is not here; he is risen! Remember how he told you while he was still with you in Galilee.

LUKE 24:5–6 (NIV)

Christ is risen!"

These triumphant words resounded from a vacated grave in A.D. 27 and the volume of their reverberations shattered every old idea of God. For Jesus not only came back from the dead, he is still alive. And his resurrection takes every definition of our living to a new level.

Why am I so excited about this? It will happen to me! My tomb will one day be as empty as his.

Do dead people come again to life? Throughout the history of the church, many dead people have been raised to life. Louis of Anjou, who died in 1297, is said to have performed some sixty-six miracles. Among them were twelve people he raised from the dead. In the Bible some eight people are raised from the dead.

One man came alive when he touched Elijah's dead bones (see 2 Kings 13:20–21). Seven more were also brought back to life. Elijah and Elisha each raised a child to life (see 1 Kings 17:19–24; 2 Kings 4:32–37). Jesus raised three people who had died during his ministry: Jairus's daughter (see Matthew 9:18–19, 23–25), the son of the widow in the city of Nain (see Luke 7:11–15), and Jesus' friend Lazarus (see John 11:1–44). The apostle Peter raised Dorcas back to life (see Acts 9:36–42), and the apostle Paul raised Eutychus, a young man who fell asleep during a sermon and fell from a third-story window to his death (see Acts 20:7–12).[17]

There have been many "near death" stories in our time and a few tales of people returning from the dead, but I have never yet heard one of these stories that has the biblical ring of truth about it. It is sometimes difficult to assess the truth of these resurrection miracles because the edges of death are hard to determine. Sometimes even doctors have been fooled in their pronunciation of genuine death. The whole idea of having wakes before funerals was to be sure that the person about to be buried was really dead. In the Middle Ages, people were sometimes pronounced dead only to be mistakenly buried alive. So the practice of a wake was born to make sure the dead really were dead.

Still, there are many near-death miracles. One (whose authenticity has been certified) is included at the end of this chapter.

But I am weary with those in our day who claim to have come back from the dead, but who yet have no proof but their own story. An example is Betty Eadie, who documented a personal experience in her bestselling book *Embraced by the Light*. She claims to have died and then returned to life four hours later. In those hours, she says, she went to heaven where she was welcomed by Jesus and shown all about the heavenly realm. Jesus then sent her back to earth.[18]

In this chapter I want to look at Jesus' resurrection and ask what this doctrine means. The resurrection serves my faith in these four ways: First, it creates in me the Christian faith. Second, it is the energy of my witness, the vitality of my worship. Third, it is the basis of all hope for my own triumph over death. Finally, it is the link to the Second Coming and therefore the basis of including myself in the ongoing, not-as-yet completed Christian story.

But the Resurrection does not stand alone. The Ascension remains attached to it. In many ways even the Second Coming must be attached. After all, the final words of the angels in Acts 1 are these: "He shall so come in like manner as you have seen him go" (Acts 1:11 NKJV).

Within this chapter I want to examine the difference between those whom Christ raised from the dead and his own resurrection. For the moment let us distinguish between the two by using the terms "resurrection" and "resuscitation". Jesus' resurrection speaks of a kind of "super life" where Christ has not merely come back alive, but also takes on a mysterious and glorious kind of life that will never end. Those Jesus raised from the dead were merely resuscitated. They came alive again but they were still as dependent on breath and pulse as ever and indeed all of them later died again.

But in the case of Jesus' resurrection, His coming to resurrected life is tied to my spiritual well being. In fact His resurrection and my salvation are cut from the same theological cloth. His return to life is the ongoing power of day-to-day vitality in my faith. It is the purpose and power behind my weekly worship. But the doctrine is even more than this. The resurrection does not merely make a dead Christ live again. It makes the living Christ my contemporary. He lives here in this world at this time with me.

I believe that most Christians have never seen His ongoing life as contemporary with their own. Most do believe Jesus walked out of the tomb, but they fail to see this event as creating a living Christ who is as alive now as they are. This Jesus is still living and inhabits their current world.

The Resurrection Creates The Christian Faith

Frank Morison was a skeptic. He decided to write a book showing how Christ's miracles were false: He was not unlike Lew Wallace, the author of *Ben Hur*, in his feelings. His goal was to strip the miraculous elements from the life of Christ and present him as he "truly was": a good teacher but not a miracle worker. Alas, his study undid his arguments. He became so wound up in the truth of the Resurrection that he wrote *Who Moved the Stone*, which has become a Christian classic in proving the Resurrection to be true. Ultimately Morison had to ask the question, where did Christianity come from? It was created when the dead Jesus became the living Christ. He—the living one—came to the race as a sign that he could regain all the territory Adam earlier lost in being cast out of Eden.

Paul sees Jesus as the second Adam (See Romans 5). And why pin the first man ever created to the best man ever to follow him? Consider this picture:

Still formed in terra-cotta clay Adam once waited for the Lord God to breathe into him the wonderful breath of life. After receiving the breath of the Creator, Adam stood and stretched, magnificently alive. For Adam the word life *did not exist since the word* death *was unknown. Such words always come in pairs. But on the dark*

*side of Eden in the wake of his sin Adam learned the whole truth.
What a dark, dark day! This is the first dream of God: Adam the
favored child is slinking out of Paradise still grasping the half
eaten fruit of his betrayal. We, like Adam, in the passing years,
must come to grips with one great inevitability: death. George
Bernard Shaw once remarked that death is the ultimate statistic—
it affects one out of one.*[19]

But there is something within my heart that cries out to be
even more and more alive. I am all caught up in what might be
called "death avoidance." As long as it is physically possible I
want to go on breathing and eating and clinging to the daylight.
I have visited the tragedies of Shakespeare again and again, but I
am never more touched than I am at the conclusion of *King Lear*,
when Lear, carrying his beautiful dead daughter back on stage
and facing the audience, cries:

*Cordelia, Cordelia! Stay a little . . .
Her voice was ever soft,
Gentle, and low, an excellent thing in woman . . .
I am old now,
And these crosses spoil me . . .
No, no, no life . . .
Why should a dog, a horse, a rat have life,
And thou no breath at all? Thou'lt come to me no more,
Never, never, never, never, never.*[20]

Yet we are all like Lear, seeing mere physical life as the great
good. But do we not know Christ? Should we not be as much
intrigued as threatened by the possibility that the world will one
day go on without us? I had a scholarly acquaintance who was

informed by his doctor that he had inoperable cancer. "You are going to die," his doctor bluntly said. The usual reply to such a diagnosis is, "How long have I got, Doc?" But my friend said, "You, too, Doc!" How true! We all live in a world where those who diagnose death are themselves living directly in the wake of their own prophecy.

I am now sixty-six years old. I know the day of my death draws ever nearer. Still, in approaching my death I cling fervently to life. For as long as I can wake to the joy of oxygen and heartbeat, I will go on putting the word *death* as far from me as I can. I once put it this way:

> *Since death is so final, most of us do all we can to avoid it. Unconsciously we learn to act in ways that guarantee our self-preservation. We keep to our side of the white line on the freeway. We strap ourselves in roller coasters. We stop, look and listen at railroad crossings. Life is dear and precautions are regular. Considering this, salvation is the most reasonable step one can take toward ultimate life, eternal self-preservation.* [21]

While I can keep alive with breath and pulse, these words say nothing about the quality of my life. But through Christ I have a higher definition of life than that which thrives on mere oxygen and nutrition. It is not enough for me to breathe; I must find some glorious reasons to do it. I do not live merely to breathe; rather I breathe to live. I may enjoy a great meal but living only to eat would soon weary my soul, which yearly grows more hungry for God than food. "Man does not live on bread alone," said Jesus (Luke 4:4).

The Resurrection is God's promise that He has given us a reason for being alive. That reason created Christianity.

The Resurrection Is The Energy of Our Faith

In the New Testament there are at least thirty-five separate references to the resurrection of Christ. Most are passive. They read like this:

- Acts 2:24 (NASB)—God raised him up . . .
- Acts 2:32 (NASB)—This Jesus God raised up . . .
- Acts 3:15 (NASB)—whom God raised from the dead . . .
- Acts 3:26 (NKJV)—God, having raised up his servant . . .

The meaning of expressing the event in the passive voice is immense. Jesus in dying put His absolute and utter faith in God.[22]

When Jane Eyre was asked by her hyper-religious headmaster if she knew where bad girls go when they die, she replied, "To Hell, Sir."

"And what do you plan to do about it?"

"I plan to live a very long time, sir."

So do we all.

Desiring to live a long time kept Spanish explorers wading around in the swamps of Florida looking for the fountain of youth. Desiring to live a long time keeps a lot of people eating oat bran when they'd rather be having hash browns. Having to die and wanting to live forever builds a strange neurosis into our lives. That neurosis is answered by the resurrection of Christ. So in a wonderful way the resurrection was God's strong step in favor of ultimate self-preservation.

If Christ's Father had not raised Him to life, He would still be dead and Matthew Arnold's awful words in *Obermann Once More* would be true:

Far hence he lies in the lorn Syrian town,
And on his grave with shining eyes,
The Syrian stars look down.

But His death was not permanent! As His Father once created human life, He has now created Easter life, and death is defeated.[23]

The resurrection is a miracle of faith within the godhead. Here the son trusted the Father when He closed His eyes in death. But in a larger sense I too must trust the Father as I approach my own hour of death. One of my most gallant friends was Ed East. I had been involved in Mr. East's conversion to Christianity. But I was unprepared for and yet have been ever so blessed by the seriousness with which he embraced Christ. I will never forget how he influenced his twin sons toward the kingdom. His boys lacked his enthusiasm for Christ, and Ed despaired of ever seeing them come to faith. Then, after several years of trying to influence them, Ed was afflicted with cancer.

This disease was most debilitating for Ed, and his boys were at first angry with God for how it seemed to them he was treating their father. But bit by bit Ed's trust in the faithfulness of God began to change his boys. They found their father, even during his most debilitating seasons of pain, always upbeat. He was never negative and always positive about how he loved God. Before he finally yielded to death both of his boys had taken up the mantle of their father's faith.

Trusting God at the moment of death is the legacy of the cross. For Jesus it spelled complete confidence, even during the immensity of His suffering. Trust at the door of death is Jesus' example of how we are to face death. God did indeed raise Jesus up from the dead and Christ at His moment of dying had put His faith entirely in God. God must be faithful or Jesus would be forever dead.

But isn't it morose to talk about death all the time? If it's not too overwhelming to consider, all world religions seem to be in place to help us deal with the idea of dying. For instance, the Bagavahd Gita—the sacred book of the Hindus—is the story of the inner wrangling of a young man asked to go to war against his soldier brother. The issue of death occasioned the writing of this sacred book. The Gilgamesh Epic is a similar tale of Gilgamesh, who wanders in despair contemplating the death of his friend Enkidu. The ancient Egyptians obviously had their fascination with death and the afterlife, as evidenced by their ornate burials. The Greek and Roman pantheons were humans' attempt to place human characteristics on the life-and-death situations that ruled their lives.

But we Christians are blessed to be able to look past death to life. The New Testament word for "resurrection" is *anastasis*.[24] This Greek word comes into English as *Anastasia*. Jesus and the resurrection becomes Christ and Anastasia, or God and Resurrection Life. There is no English word that really translates *anastasis*. The most elementary meaning of the word is to "stand again!"[25]

In Oklahoma during the days of my childhood I lived a very odd idiom. People would often say of a recuperating friend, "He's up and about!" This is the Oklahoma way of saying *"Anastasis!"* This is the cry by which God revived the disconsolate friends of Christ. He is risen! *Anastasis!* He's up and about!

Do dead men stand again? One dead man did, and when He did, He authenticated the notion that others might do it, too. I have grieved in black cars that idled along after hearses, and as I followed these dank vehicles I pondered Job's question: If a man dies will he live again? How important is *Anastasis?*

"What was the new life that Christ introduced to the world really like? Substance that allowed Him to eat fish (see Luke

24:42) but also vanish (see Luke 24:31). He was physical enough to have scars (see John 20:27), but so ethereal that He went up in a cloud out of sight (see Acts 1:9). He was so substantial that He could cook breakfast by the sea (see John 21:9), but so lacking in physical density that He could enter a room that had every door locked (see John 20:19). After the brutality of crucifixion, the resurrection shouted out the glorious immutability of Christ."[26]

Paul talked of a moment when "corruptibility must put on incorruption" (1 Corinthians 15:53). The resurrection doesn't just change the inside out. It is our great transformer and it changes us from the outside in. Corruptibility is infused with incorruption. Or, to put it more honestly, decomposition is ordered to "stop it." Death is swallowed up by life. Decomposition is forever over. Now no life is subject to decay. We live forever and our new life derives from His life. He's up and about and we are infused with undiminished vitality.

We have passed that time in our faddish culture where everyone seemed to be confessing some near-death experience. But Dr. Willliam Ritchie confessed to one that actually made *Guidepost* magazine. He told about the time when he was on the way home from medical school for a much needed midterm study break. He was seized by an uncontrollable spasm of coughing on the train and this spasm ultimately sent him into a seizure. He blacked out. During this period of darkness, he was visited first by a bright light which turned out to be a "personage." This "person" who appeared to him reminded him of God's purpose for his life. When he woke up—some hours later—he was in a hospital room.

After a brief period of convalescence, he grew strong enough to visit the hospital records room and there in a file folder found his own death certificate, signed by the attending physician. He had died of double-lobar pneumonia and remains to this day the only person whose death remains certified by courthouse records.

But it is not merely these things that convince me of the truth of his testimony. I am motivated to believe by the fact that he testifies it has been his life-long objective to get back with that "personage" who visited him and changed the value system of his life. He has—since that experience—used his life to serve others in the interest of the one who visited him during his illness. This makes all of life throb with excitement.

Indeed it is the Resurrection that makes our worship throb with excitement. How often on Easter do I go to church and find myself participating in the delirium of the occasion? The church is mad with joy. I join the madness. But where does this madness come from? It comes from that first delirium, when the women arrive at Jesus' tomb to find it empty. They could not contain themselves. His life became the vitality of their worship. It is still the vitality of ours.

But this Resurrection vitality does not occur just on Easter. The Christian worship time was set upon Sunday. The Jews (and nearly all of the early Christians were Jews) always worshiped on the Sabbath—the seventh day, the day of rest. But early Christians picked Sunday, the first day of the week, for this was the day of the week on which Jesus rose from the dead. Easter was the annual celebration of His Resurrection, but Sunday was the "week-i-versary" of His return to life. Every week the Resurrection is to be the focus and energy of our worship. Shouldn't we all wish to feel the glory of Easter each week?

His Triumph Over Death Is the Basis of *Our* Hope of Triumphing Over Death

Jesus demonstrated that Easter life keeps two things straight. First, resurrection is not merely spiritual; the body is involved. Second, it is not merely a bodily proposition. A dead body come alive again is at worst a zombie and at best a resuscitation. Resurrection is different. Jesus' life imparts to me a confidence that my approaching death will be no more permanent than His was. He rose. Because He did it, I will, too.

During Jesus' own life, He resurrected other people from the dead, although, as I mentioned before, it really isn't accurate to use the word *resurrection* with Lazarus or the widow's son in Nain. There is no question that they were dead and restored to life. Still, once they did come back alive they were as dependent on pulse, nutrition, and respiration as they had ever been. Not so with Christ! Further, the widow's son at Nain and Lazarus himself had to go through the ordeal of dying all over again.[27]

This is not to deny there was once a moment of majesty in Bethany. For Lazarus had died. There was no doubt about it! When Jesus asked to see his resting place, and orders the stone over his grave to be rolled away, Martha protested, "Lord, he has been dead four days, by this time he stinketh" (see John 11:39).

But Jesus ordered the dead man to come forth. And he did. I've always tried to imagine how Lazarus must have felt. Whatever his state of bliss, he heard coming through the mists, the bell-like voice of the Messiah. "Lazarus." Out Lazarus came. He was slammed from a glorious stupor into the hard reality of the cave, from the bright-white light of glory to the damp darkness of odd odors—his own. And mingling with the acrid smell of *rigor-mortis* was the close scent of thick spices and old blood.

"Come forth, Lazarus."

Hut . . . two . . . three . . . here he came!

Jesus wept (John 11:35 KJV). Why? Maybe because he had summoned a good friend from the resplendence of eternity back to dull times. Lazarus had been called to leave a better world for a worse one. He was being summoned from life back to death, from joy back to pain, from the bright presence of God to the dingy illumination of the planet.

No wonder Jesus wept.

The miracle of life. The tension I feel in always being alive lies in knowing I will not always be alive. From the moment I was born I was caught up in the process of dying. But death is an obscure territory. I can never know exactly what lies just across its borders. The only thing I must face is the issue of my not being here anymore. I'm not fond of trying to imagine the world without me!

So far the only death in my immediate family I have experienced is the death of my mother. I will never forget the power and exhilaration I felt when the attending pastor read the words of 1 Corinthians 15:51–57 (NIV):

> Listen, I tell you a mystery: We will not all sleep, but we will all be changed—in a flash, in the twinkling of an eye, at the last trumpet. For the trumpet will sound, the dead will be raised imperishable, and we will be changed. For the perishable must clothe itself with the imperishable, and the mortal with immortality. When the perishable has been clothed with the imperishable, and the mortal with immortality, then the saying that is written will come true: "Death has been swallowed up in victory."
>
> "Where, O death, is your victory? Where, O death, is your sting?"

The sting of death is sin, and the power of sin is the law. But thanks be to God! He gives us the victory through our Lord Jesus Christ.

After serving for twenty-six years in one church, I resigned my pastorate to go teach in the seminary. As pastor of a large church my social calendar had been full. My influence in a huge seminary was less than I imagined it would be. So shortly after I arrived, I found myself somewhat depressed. Nobody knew me. I had gone from being the center of community esteem to anonymity. I moved from a world where I was visible to one in which I was invisible. I moved from a world where I mattered to one in which my presence was inconsequential.

I think that is why we fear death. We are not so much afraid of burning in fire as we hate thinking of our beautiful world going on without us. It was Emily Dickinson who wrote, "Because I could not stop for death, he kindly stopped for me. The carriage held but just ourselves and immortality!" Ah yes, Emily has our number: Death is a lonely carriage ride and the carriage takes us off down a dark road where dank moss drapes from twisted boughs hiding the world of light just beyond the mist.

Yet we may have over-rated our importance in the world. We are gone from being Mr. Nobody to being Mr. Anonymous. Emily also wrote: "I'm nobody, who are you—are you nobody too?" Death we hate partially because it is a journey of self-awareness to the fear of a terrifying nonexistence.

The resurrection is more than the central miracle of Christianity; it is also the one act of God that assures me that Christ can never become obsolete. "He is risen" does not mean that He came alive again just for the men of that long-ago day. It means that He is alive forevermore and that He is literally my own living

Savior contemporary with my generation. Paul could call Him friend. Jerome too. Likewise He was the living companion of Augustine, St. Francis, John Wycliffe, Thomas More, Charles Wesley, and Dwight Moody. The Resurrection means that He has become the great contemporary of every generation—mine, too!

Miracle of miracles! I am on a pilgrimage of life. As my forebears sang that they were en route to "a land that is fairer than day, and by faith they could see it afar," so I join their testimony. Many times now I have been to the gravesides of lost loved ones. There I face the great light of Easter. This life miracle camps at the center of my soul and reminds me: I will live forever. I shall be like Him. I shall make Easter life my own and as the Apostle promises, "So shall I ever be with the Lord."

The Resurrection–Ascension Comes Attached To the Doctrine of the Second Coming

The coupling of these two doctrines—the Resurrection and Ascension—occurred on the Mount of Ascension when the angels said to the mortals: "Men of Galilee," "why do you stand here looking into the sky? This same Jesus, who has been taken from you into Heaven, will come back in the same way you have seen him go into heaven (Acts 1:10–11 NIV)."

Jesus rose even as Heaven announced he would be back! Therefore the resurrection has become the *sine qua non*—"that without which something would not be what it is"—of Christianity; without it the hope of His Second Coming could not exist. The victory of Easter is but the promised victory for which the church still waits.

Yet he had to be made alive at Easter for this ultimate victory to occur. In 1963 laying the foundation for a new YMCA in

Jerusalem, a skeleton was found. It was a crucified skeleton about two thousand years old. Scientists who unearthed these bones said this man had a large forehead and was super-intelligent. Of course the implication—fueled by the skeptics of Christianity— was that this "smart, dead guy" was Jesus. But this was no real evidence of Jesus' body. It was only clear evidence that sometimes smart guys get crucified.

In 1970 a second crucified skeleton was found and this one still had nails in his hands, fanning the skeptics' fires. But too many skeletons are as hard on a skeptic's arguments as too few. As John Osborne's Luther, fighting his war against venerating sacred relics, said, "How does it happen of Jesus' twelve disciples, eighteen of them are now buried in Germany?" It is a good question. We must ever contend for it because only a living Jesus can be a coming Jesus.

Conclusion

The miracle of the Resurrection is clearly the King of Miracles. It is so foundational to faith that its truth authenticates all other miracles and gives Christianity life. No wonder Paul said, "And if Christ has not been raised, our preaching is useless and so is your faith (1 Corinthians 15:14 NIV)."

Yes, there is always some question about whether faith creates miracles or miracles, faith. But in the case of the Resurrection this problem is easily resolved. The Resurrection occurred before there was any Christianity and had it never occurred, there never would have been.

So in a book of this sort, which is set to waken the world to the reality of miracles, I must turn to the empty tomb and shout, "There is but one source of miracle." Every mute who ever woke to singing, every cripple who learned to leap and run, every blind soul who woke to the wonder of a sunrise must bring the joy of their healing to the garden tomb and say, "Only when he conquered death did my poor body find its life."

The power that raised Christ from the dead has taught me to recite as my own this wondrous litany of mystery. He lives. I live. His life is enough to heal my dying. It is a balm for the smaller wounds of my living. And in the end I will step into the new life.

CHAPTER FIVE

Miracles: God Talking Back to a Scientific Age

*Most of the time the fact that this fact is impossible doesn't
bother me. I live by the impossible. Like the White Queen, I find it
a good discipline to practice believing as many as seven
impossible things every morning before breakfast."*
MADELEINE L'ENGLE

One should not stand at the foot of a sick person's bed, because that spot is reserved for the guardian angel."[28] This profound Jewish proverb seems so quaint when one considers that most sick people lie in hospital beds surrounded by oscilloscopes, IV's, defribulators, monitors, etc. It is an ominous picture that entangles guardian angels in the lines and cords of medical technology. Where good science and great miracles are both free to exist, they create a better life. So pray for any illness you may have, but when your prayer is finished, rise from your knees and call a doctor.

"The world's changed with the grandeur of God," wrote Gerard Manley Hopkins. I couldn't agree more; Even a tadpole in a glass jar speaks of God to me. But the next line of his poem reads, "It will flame out like shining shook from foil." Hopkins' "tinfoil" metaphor makes me wonder if I could ever define the power of God without casting it in some technological metaphor like tin foil or some Ziploc concept of technology.

Day by day technology performs a million miracles, yet these miracles can all be rationally explained. Scientists are the new magi, the new miracle workers, and while the cyber-rabbits they pull out of their virtual hats are as logical as binary mathematics, I still gasp at their miracles.

Some scientists appear to have outgrown their need for God. But here and there a few appear to be on my side. "The most beautiful thing we can experience is the mysterious," said Albert Einstein.[29] Was this super-scientist not saying, "There is a point at which the most superb "wow!" scientists can produce is followed by the hush of a million marvels that defy science to even speak.

How does one tap into the mystery that lies beyond science? By praying, perhaps. But the super-technologists would say "No!"

I once knew a doctor who was an atheist. "How do you operate on believers, who given the choice, would prefer you to believe in God?"

"I am a man of good science," he told me. "When I have done the best to apply my science, the outcome is in the hands of science. I would rather trust this to heal than count on some nebulous, mysterious working force."

I made a mental note to choose another surgeon.

Prayer works best where science and faith are friends. Joan Wester Anderson reports this:

In a 1988 double-blind study at the University of California, San Francisco, cardiologists randomly divided 393 hospitalized heart patients into two groups. One was prayed for (by volunteers who did not know them), the other was not. The patients who received prayer had less complications and needed less medical intervention. In a recent Virginia poll, over 14% of adults said they had been healed either by prayer or a divine source.[30]

Since God is the author of good science I believe we must always bind scientific wisdom with God's mysterious power.

So as we venture into this chapter let us be prepared to learn to think about miracles in a way that sets them free from all our biases. Let us honestly admit that we are postmodern thinkers and have lost what premoderns felt when they encountered a true miracle. Those who lived long ago had no backlog of scientific super-conditioning to get over. God was bigger than the world of human logic. To this day miracles still occur most frequently when people believe they are possible.

Technology and Miracle

The major stumbling block to our credulity may be that we have been "wowed!" by our own technology to the point that we can't look on the simple wonders of Scripture and not be underwhelmed. We have amazed ourselves with everything from cloning embryos to fish that talk from battery-operated wall plaques. Why is merely walking on the water to be esteemed when we have the Cypress Gardens Slalom competitions? We seemed to have out-"wowed!" the simpler more primitive wonders of Scripture.

We have fortunately moved beyond the place where the alchemists and theologians of the Middle Ages viewed nature as

God's armor and weaponry to contend with us. Hurricanes, earthquakes, and typhoons were once thought to be the thunderbolts of Jehovah. According to this view, when God wearied with a nation, he merely laid a bacteria of some sort on a nameless plate, and sat back to watch the Plague decimate his world.

From such a preposterous view of nature, scientists who drained swamps or put up lightning rods were seen to be the adversaries of God. After all, if God wishes to strike a rebellious church with lightning, should he be thwarted by a lightning rod from doing His will? Should Galveston build a sea wall if God wishes to flog the city with hurricanes? By such thinking the Corps of Engineers becomes an army of anti-God militants thwarting God's eternal purposes with flood control.

Perhaps in our day quarrels over abortion, birth control, and, certainly, evolution often stem from this fact-versus-truth debate. Evolutionists have a way of arrogantly sneering at creationists. And some Christians stoop to cheap tricks instead of real arguments. Sometimes orthodoxy gets cute to avoid the necessity of sound argument. In *Inherit the Wind*, Brady cried against the geologists that he was more interested in the *Rock of Ages* than he was the ages of rocks. There's a church marquee in my neighborhood that recently read, "Evolution is science fiction."

It has been hard for Christians in our day to find out exactly what they believe because within Christianity there is a great division about the nature of miracles. Many churchgoers no longer consider them to be true. When theologians argue, who can be trusted? Some liberal "scholars" who deny miracles believe that hell is nothing more than the "fiery, swelling ignorance" of the Bible Belt. Some fundamentalists believe it not only exists but it is located directly beneath the basement floor of an ivy-league divinity school!

How Technology Redefined the Word *Miracle*

Technology did not set out to redefine miracles. It just continued doing impressive and unbelievable things, so that the unusual became the ordinary. Moses created a wall of water at the Red Sea. So did the Corps of Engineers at Hoover Dam. Jesus once walked on water. Now we have the Cypress Garden Water Show. Both Elijah and the Wright Brothers flew.

There is no real conflict between technology and miracle, but because of technology we are not so easily awed today. One often imagines how George Washington would react if he could be taken from his day and dropped in the middle of ours. The shock would likely overwhelm him. We have exactly the reverse problem. Technology has so overwhelmed us that simple miracles underwhelm us. We have gotten used to bread that browns itself, houses that regulate their own temperature, and ships that orbit the planet in a mere ninety minutes. General Washington would have been struck dumb by the window-box full of little people that we call television.

The fact is when too many unbelievable things are happening, everything becomes believable. Edward Jenner's smallpox vaccine saved more people from disease in a month than Jesus did in his entire life. Yet Jenner's vaccine is considered good science, and not miraculous. Technology unintentionally did something worse than diminish miracles. Like an egotistic Roman emperor, it proclaimed its own deity. Technology became at once the grand savior and the great enslaver.

Communication theorist Marshall McLuhan's Global Village vision was not without its altar. Technology was the totem, and it demanded worship. McLuhan's idol was a high-tech god whose electronic giggle was set off by the plunger of the toaster. This god taught us to pray, "Give us this day, our daily toast." It cried out behind the towrope of the power launch as it strapped on its skis, "Lord, if it be you, bid me come to you on the water." It spoke from Sesame Street and said, "Let the little children come unto me and forbid them not." It said from every computer reel, "Why keep all these things and ponder them in your heart? Give them to a soft-disc system." It cried its technological atonement from the Red Cross Bloodmobile, "Without the shedding of blood, you have no life—AB or O positive!"

I find it hard not to worship a superb technology crammed with miracles. Our near-miraculous technology seems to lord it over my own dependence on a miraculous God. For one thing, technology makes no demands on my morality. I cannot have the miracle of a new heart without being submitted to the domination of Jesus Christ as Lord. But I can have the miracle of heart surgery and repudiate both God and technology.

Technology: The New "Amoral" God

Technology itself is not a major stumbling block to my faith in Christ. It is how we manipulate that technology that concerns me. In his final book, *The Demon-Haunted World*, Carl Sagan said most Americans believe the earth has been visited at least once by alien beings. This kind of statement really says how far Westerners believe in the achievement of technology and how far they are willing to go to replace Christ with fanciful new theories. I am amazed at how fanciful those theories get.

Erich Von Däniken pushed forward Sagan's notion to the ridiculous. He saw Christ as an alien and therefore viewed Jesus' incarnation as a planetary visit, and saw nothing wrong with suggesting that Christ arrived on the planet by UFO to announce

God's involvement in the world: "The news that Jesus was an astronaut has been haunting the press and relevant literature for some time, like the Loch Ness monster, sometimes accepted, sometimes dismissed.The inventor of the latest Jesus cult is the Soviet philologist Dr. Vyatcheslav Saitsev of the University of Minsk. Saitsev believes that Jesus came from outer space, that he was a representative of a higher civilization, and that would partially explain his supernatural powers and abilities."[31]

L. Ron Hubbard, the father of Scientology, also held to such odd notions, blending his Jesus with "spacey theology." And who can forget, when the comet Hale Bopp passed our solar system, the cult members who committed suicide in an attempt to join their souls with those interstellar forces.

The psychological revolution that accompanied the rise of technology not only abandoned the biblical definitions of Christ, it altered also the biblical definitions of man. We were forced to find our identity in the dialogue of psychologists who seemed rarely to agree on how we could locate the shortest route to meaning. Removing sin was a matter of conditioning or adjustment. The "I'm OK—You're OK" movement is a new way of viewing our depravity and living with it. Followers of psychologist B. F. Skinner overlooked the protest of ethics and dealt with setting us free of all moral requirements. For most, traditional psychiatry seemed an endless therapy that never healed. Innovative psychiatry, on the other hand, was spastic and experimental. Technology had its greatest psychological impact in the creation of altered states. Uppers and downers, legally or illegally dispensed, were creating fields of moods.

But psychology itself, like other sciences, has not fulfilled its promises. Pure science will never fulfill, for it pursues facts alone. The great issues of meaning lie always with truth. We cannot castigate those who follow facts and create a magnificent world of technological miracle—they often make life easier and safer. But we can say to them, "You have not gone far enough. Come with us to Christ who is the epicenter of meaning and who once told the world he was the very truth of God."

Beyond Technology to Useable Truth!

The world of believers will see miracle as most possible when they remember that the greatest of all miracles is still the one most accessible to all: the miracle of the new birth. Being born again is useable truth. When believers understand that they have this miracle and have long taken its glory for granted, they will be far less likely to be awed by technology.

We are thrown back against mystery and its necessity to add real meaning to our technologically centered lives. The late J. B. Phillips confesses that such a mystery invaded his world shortly after C. S. Lewis died. He used this story to deal very strongly with the notion that Jesus' Resurrection was more real than even the phenomenon he was describing. Speaking of Lewis, he wrote:

But the late C. S. Lewis, whom I did not know very well and had only seen in the flesh once, but with whom I had corresponded a fair amount, gave me an unusual experience. A few days after his death, while I was watching television, he "appeared" sitting in a chair within a few feet of me, and spoke a few words which were particularly relevant to the difficult circumstances through which I was passing. He was ruddier in complexion than ever, grinning all over his face and, as the old-fashioned saying has it, positively glowing with health. The interesting thing to me was that I had not been thinking of him at all . . . He was just there—"large as life and twice as natural!" A week later, this time when I was in bed reading before going to sleep, he appeared again, even more rosily radiant than before, and repeated to me the same message, which was very important to me at the time . . . The reason I mention this personal and memorable experience is that although "Jack Lewis" was real, in a certain sense, it did not occur to me that I should reach out and touch him. It is possible that some of the appearances of the risen Jesus were of this nature . . . but the writers of the Gospels, in their naïve unselfconscious way make it plain that something much more awesome and indeed authoritative characterized Christ's infallible proofs.[32]

We Christians do gape at the glory of science. This is not wrong. But we need to broaden our wonder, until they can see that ours is a world full of God-possibilities that no science can duplicate.

Perhaps we could begin with viewing our own conversions as miraculous. If only we could admit to this, the whole world of God's other unexplainable things will suddenly become accessible to them. I think it is generally true that children view their conversions in a more romantic and emotional and miraculous way than do adults. For many adults their conversion is often seen more matter-of-factly, as in "joining the church" or "going through membership-induction classes."

The wonders of science can never supply me with the meaning I get from grace, and grace itself is the best of miracles. The Atonement comes steeped in the mystery of its greatest question: "How can one man die for all the people?" Who can say? But this mystery is not only the heart of my faith, it is the heart of all miracles. Mystery leaves me asking *how?* I see Christ's miracles but I don't understand them. But as my maturity has grown I quit asking *how* God redeems us, and start asking *why?* I have been "miraclized" by grace. Therefore there is little use in my asking *how* God does anything. Even if he answered me, I could never understand it. But what I cannot understand deepens my intrigue. I am mixed up with God in a wonderful and warm addiction. This is a better wonder than technology. This wonder keeps me running to God for daily miracles. Once He gives me the wonder I crave, I am ever more deeply lost in the mystery that both "wows!" and saves me.

The Reality That Surpasses Science

During the Indonesian Revival, many miracles were reported as they happened in and around the jungles of Indonesia. American missionaries returned to America with fantastic tales. Healings were frequent, as were miracles of other sorts. But no miracle worker told such tales with more acceptance than Mel Tari.

Mr. Tari arrived in Los Angeles and became an immediate object of interest among American evangelicals. Where burned the revival fire of Indonesia, he said, healings, exorcisms, even resurrections were frequent. He reported stories of Christians walking on the water in Indonesia. While American evangelicals seemed eager to lap up his miracle stories, his acceptance all too soon waned. I had trouble deciding if Mr. Tari's tales were too fantastic to be believed or if American evangelicals, long tempered by scientific thinking, just had trouble believing him. I do believe that miracles are more readily accepted in animistic culture than in technocracies.

But that does raise a very legitimate question: How does God best talk to a technology-driven age? Through miracles? No? Then how? Miracles are not to be trusted alone. God's revelation of himself in Scripture is the ultimate of truth.

Time and again the world has set Science against Scripture. Yet Scripture holds sway on the Christian mind, for the Bible reports the existence of miracles. Still, the Bible exalts written authority over the authority of signs and wonders. The Reformers went so far as to say that miracles ceased at the end of the biblical era because the world was not enmeshed in magic and miracles. They wanted a return to Scripture that would provide a strong base for faith and not let the faith get lost in the thoughtless excitement that went with the pursuit of dreams, wonders, and miracles.

Alchemy was in some ways the precurser to modern science. The churches were the first laboratories of "science." Yet the alchemists rarely pursued science for its own sake. They were giddy with the notion that they could create an elixir of youth, by which those who drank would live forever. Some of them were also convinced that if the world waited long enough they could transmute lead into gold.

Coupled with this "primitive science" they developed odd doctrines that were hardly scientific but that enslaved the gullible into believing visions and wonders could be purchased. This was the logic behind the selling of indulgences and the praying of souls out of purgatory. Johann Tetzel offended Martin Luther with his sale of indulgences. The poor often spent their last on these unverifiable "miracle workers." Tetzel took their money saying, "As soon as the coin in the copper rings, the soul from purgatory springs." The Church was itself corrupt enough to encourage such indulgence, for the money collected from the abused poor was being used to build St. Peters in Rome. So the coffers of the church were best filled by keeping such superstitions alive.

And the Alchemists worked on. The uninformed people of the Middle Ages bought their tokens, convinced they were helping souls enter heaven. But miracles point to the fact that we never lost our place in paradise, as far as the love of our Maker is known. God gives us miracles not to show off, but because he loves us too much to see us hurt or be puzzled about his reality or live under the heel of Satan. Hence miracle. When there is no ordinary natural way to proclaim His love the miracle calls us back to the remembrance of Eden. There, where we walked with Him in the cool of the day, we never doubted. His love was His presence, and His presence—after all—is the greatest of miracles.

But still we often seem so lost on a dry scientific odyssey through a desert of technology. We ask ourselves, "Did Jesus really do anything all that fantastic? Did He walk on the water? I have skied on it. Did He calm the storm? I have a friend who sees hurricanes. Did He give sight? My doctor does corneal transplants. Did He speak to five thousand at a time? I have satellite-driven cable networks. Did alien beings talk with Jesus on the Mount of Transfiguration? I have seen it happen in every Lucas and Spielberg movie."

We are the cyber-space people. Everything we do would have looked miraculous to Simon Peter. The difference is that we can explain our miracles to ourselves and so we are no longer intrigued by our wonders. But in explaining our miracles, we have become only the "special effects" culture. Once the heart-transplant tells the world *how* he downloads his e-mail while flying in his Lear, he must confess his all-too-explainable miracles have furnished him no meaning, for they are too void of mystery. Technology at first dulls us to biblical miracles. Finally, technology at last dulls us to it's own wondrous accomplishments.

We must continually seek to safeguard ourselves from the wiles of technology. No, the feeding of the five thousand cannot be replaced by a massive Somali Red-Cross air-lift program. Both are compassionate, but only in the wonder of the loaves is the God of miracles involved. We must have Jesus. We must sit and eat real fish created from thin air and feel the thrill of great power furnishing us our daily bread. Any other kind of bread is too explainable—too void of mystery to really feed us. For what we need is not the bread that perishes but the bread that nourishes us with God's unexplainable power.

The Freedom of God

A major theme of this book is that miracles come as God's special evidence that we have a special meaning to God. When God grants a miracle to save us or get us out of some pickle, we must admit he would not have done it if He didn't love us. (Of course, His predictability is also a way He says He loves us. So when we ask for a miracle and it doesn't arrive, we must yet praise Him for the natural law that makes all our lives possible.) He wouldn't have done it unless we had some special meaning to Him. But there is one other reason that He does it: He demonstrates that He will not act in any way that imprisons Him in His own system.

Human significance lies behind the whole Passover miracle, but the freedom of God is also at stake. It wasn't Moses who said, "Let my people go!" It was God. God acted in the interest of human freedom, for He Himself is free. He cannot be imprisoned in the natural world.

Chesterton was right when he said that a universe with no possibility of miracles imprisons God in the system:

A miracle only means the liberty of God. The traditional church believed that man and God both had a sort of spiritual freedom. Calvinism took away the freedom from man, but left it to God. Scientific materialism binds the Creator Himself; it chains up God as the Apocalypse chained the devil. It leaves nothing free in the universe.[33]

And Deists make God their captive by allowing Him to create the universe but not be involved in it. God was once extraordinary (as when He created), they said, but He no longer does anything extraordinary.

The problem arises when we encounter the tales of miracles that sound magical or fanciful or perhaps even silly. Part of my problems with the so-called miracles that occur in the *Pseudepigrapha* (false Bible books) is that they are full of fanciful stories that challenge the credulity of the modern mind. This is even true of some of the Apocrypha. There are stories in the "Rest of Daniel" or the "Rest of Esther" that have unbelievable things happening. In the books of 1 and 2 Infancy—books that purport to be the account of Jesus' missing childhood years—there are a great many such stories. Jesus in one of these accounts orders a snake who has killed a child to crawl out of its hole and 'refang' the dead boy and withdraw its venom from the child. The snake obeys and the child comes back to life. In another such story Jesus—like the children He plays with—makes birds out of clay, but His birds (unlike the less sophisticated birds of the other children) fly away upon being created.

These same kind of fanciful stories pervade the lives of the saints. Francis Xavier's life stories include many such tales as this one:

> *We were at sea . . . when a violent storm arose which alarmed the crew. Xavier drew from his bosom a small crucifix, which he always carried about him, and leaned overboard, intending to dip it into sea: but the crucifix dropped out of his hand, and immediately disappeared. It was manifest that this loss much affected him . . . Later Francis and I were walking on the shore . . . We had proceeded about five-hundred paces, when we perceived a crab fish coming from the sea, and bearing, suspended in his claws— the identical crucifix that was lost. I saw the crab approach the Father, and stop before him . . . I joined Francis in returning thanks to God for so evident a miracle.*[34]

So in looking at what miracle means, it is immediately clear that some miracles are too fantastic to hold place alongside the key miracles of the New Testament, or even the most reasonable contemporary acts of God. Clearly all miracles do not share the same significance. Perhaps this is why the Reformers all objected to the bath of contemporary signs and wonders in which the Reformation came to be. But both the Reformers—and all great scholars—would agree that the miracles of Scriptures cannot be done without.

It is unfortunate that not all contemporary scholars have kept faith with the Reformers in this matter. In denying God things such as the power to resurrect Christ, they deny God the freedom to live above nature and beyond reason.

Surely our tiny thinking is a narrow cell for a cosmic God. Believing in miracles sets God free to work in any way He wishes. Yes, God's freedom can at times seem harsh. God set Israel free by killing the first-born of all of Egypt. At Jericho many Canaanites died when the walls collapsed. But if God does not appear gracious to all, we must remember that He acts for reasons that cannot always be seen without the perspectives of time and destiny.

If God is free, He can go any direction He wishes to accomplish his ends. He may either tamper with the taste buds of the wedding guests so they think the water is wine, or He may in fact change well-water to port. When the prophet is hungry the ravens bring him food. He could just as easily have multiplied his last loaf of bread indefinitely. When the mob is hungry, God may multiply the bread or He may as easily send a flock of ravens to bring food.

Of course, so often miracles tend to get confused with coincidence. When the Israelites were dying of hunger someone likely said, "The quails just happened to be flying over Sinai. It's our lucky day!" Perhaps when they sat down to dinner that night, someone else remarked how fortunate they were to be in the flyway of a million quail. But someone else may have been just as convinced that God mercifully sent the birds.

The important thing to remember is that the Bible contains from first to last the tale of God's miraculous acts in human history. Each time God acted He said that we have special meaning to Him. With every miracle we gained a new quality of life that taught us how special we are. The Lord of the universe is our special, redeeming friend.

Conclusion

I'm afraid we moderns have lost sight of the power of the mystery and miracle. Further, we may have lost sight of how our personal prayer life may play a part in God's redemptive miracles.

In July of 1881 President James Garfield became the second American president to fall to an assassin's bullet. Charles Giuteau, a political "crazy," was the assassin. However, Garfield's death was different from Lincoln's some fifteen years earlier. Garfield lingered on for months between the time he was shot and the time he actually died. During those months the best of the nation's doctors tried to save him. But the most wonderful of circumstances accompanied these months of struggle. America became united in an ever-widening circle of prayer. The focus was intense. Some might say it was to no avail, for on September nineteenth the president died.[35] Yet prayer is to some extent its own reward, and it is a prime indicator that those who pray honestly believe that the God of miracles may be entreated for His special help in a time of special need.

Could such a concerted prayer effort happen today? September 11, 2001, says that it can. Still the brief flurry of devotion that accompanied September 11 makes it seem that America as a whole may have lost her confidence in supernatural solutions to national crises.

But have modern churchgoers lost sight of the world of miracle? While church attendance booms in America, most suburbanite Christians have incarcerated God in a box where they worship Him but never really see much of Him. We sing to God. We even pray to Him asking Him to make God well, but in a sense science is our real faith. Arthur Guiterman rightly assessed our worship of science and education when he wrote $E=MC^2$:

Come little lad, come little lass
Your docile creed recite.
We know that energy equals mass,
By the square of the speed of light.

When we have prayed, it's okay with us if God does or not involve himself in our affairs. After all, He's not the God He once was before we could use technology to do so many things on our own. Right?

I think I first felt God being lessened by technology thirty years ago when Philip Blaiburg, a South African man, became the world's first successful heart transplant. I remember his picture on the front of news magazines; he held a beaker of solution containing his own heart. The photo inspired fear and wonder around the world. But Christian Bernard, his surgeon, was catapulted into instant fame.

I realized then that we live in a world where science can hold the world so in awe that all of us ask, "God, where are you? And what shall be our worship? Who is to get the credit for life when it is extended in the operating room? And what of tent revivals or cable television miracles?"

I long to hear Einstein's benediction once again: "Come let us see that the universe is mysterious." Then maybe we can say God is yet in charge. Miracles stand gathered in armies ready to storm the citadels of haughty human pride. Heaven is merely waiting for the human race to see things its way.

CHAPTER SIX

Miracles: The Gift of a Holy Life to a Less Holy World

More things are wrought by prayer than this world dreams of.
ALFRED, LORD TENNYSON

At the center of God's phenomenal and unexplainable events there exists a holy life. At the center of all miracles is a miracle worker who lives an unworldly or other-worldly life.

Those who take their sin seriously are probably those who most often see God heal others. Author Douglas Connelly once said, "We should examine our hearts carefully when sickness comes upon us. If we are walking in disobedience in some area, we should confess the sin and make whatever changes God directs us to make. I sometimes encourage sick people to allow the Spirit of God to search their hearts."[36] This does not mean all sick people suffer because of sin. Nor does it mean the healthy are righteous. But there is a mighty correlation between sin and sickness.

Further, righteous living is accounted unto the holy life as a kind of power. Who can say why, exactly. Perhaps because God so esteems the love that prompts holy living.

When I was a sophomore in college, Jim Elliott and his four companions became missionary martyrs on the banks of the Curarary River in Ecuador. The whole world was touched by their martyrdom. But it was only after the publication of Elisabeth Elliott's *Through Gates of Splendor* that the whole world encountered the holy living of Jim Elliott. As I read that book and its sequel *Under the Shadow of the Almighty* I came to feel the heavy but delicious weight of glory.

Martyrs do not die primarily because the world is against them. They die because they are so in love with God they have no choice about how they will either spend their lives or end their lives. Indeed, to spend or end is one and the same with them; all is done in obedience to Christ. They turn from all notions of praise for their heroism. It is Jesus, and not their own commitment, that is to be glorified. Still, without their commitment Jim and his group would never have come to the heroism that left the world in awe. This same thing may be said of authentic miracles. Those who perform them do not tout their own glory. They serve a different reason to be.

The kind of devotion that keeps a miracle worker alive usually focuses on four ideas. I do not offer these in any particular order of importance for they are all important to those who serve a living savior. But they are four in number. First, humility. This is the loss of the importance of our personal identity in the attempt to serve God's will. Second, communion. Something happens when men and woman who are hungry for Jesus taste the wine and bread. They are often given the power to change their world. Further, they see at once the clarity and importance of merging the sacred and the secular worlds. Third, asceticism. Every saint is bound by the descriptions of self-denial. They become ascetics refusing to indulge themselves in rich living and hungering for the spartan life of self-denial. Finally, they are eager to find Christ through any avenue of service God offers them.

Humility: The Gift of Seeing Our Importance Set Next to God's

The refusal to see ourselves as highly significant in the service of Christ is the first evidence that we are at least interested in pursuing true humility. Mark 1 forces me to posit Jesus' "tell no man" against the riotous applause of current cable television miracle workers. When I compare the two, a huge credibility gap is exposed. In a previous decade I had a church member who desired to have all the experience the Holy Spirit desired for him. He had no sickness to be miraculously cured of, yet in his mind he felt that if he could just be "slain in the spirit" he would be graced by the power that attends this kind of ultimate experience. He believed he would have a new and miraculous infilling of God. He spent a great deal of money traveling to a distant city to be touched by the greatest "spirit-slayer" of the day.

Just as he desired, he was slain in the spirit and according to him was filled with new power. In fact, in our congregation, where being spirit slain was not a thing to be coveted, he could often be found at the hub of Bible study groups telling of the wonder of his new experience. Having observed the miracle worker who gave him this experience, I found it hard to tell who was least humble, the curer or the cured. As this man bragged of his experience he seemed to talk less and less of Christ.

Conversely, true humility was shown by people such as Anthony of the Desert—known as the founder of monasticism— who was most desirous that people never see himself as a miracle worker. All true miracles were of Christ, he said. Christ alone was the miracle worker. To elevate any other human to that office was a kind of blasphemy. Given the fact that Anthony was ever at war with Satan it is easy to understand why he believed that Satan was the prince of both pride and illusion.

Anthony fought with demons all his life. When he died in 356 C.E. (at the age of 106) it was said angels formed a barricade of glory all around his gravesite. Anthony fits the image of humility. His holy life not only worked many miracles but also commanded an honor guard of angels at his passing.

Anthony's life teaches me that the Bible is replete with Satan's counterfeit wonders, or antimiracles. And as I said earlier, to the spiritually untrained heart Satan's "miracles" can appear as outstanding as God's. Remember Moses' rod that God changed into a snake? The Egyptian miracle workers could perform the same miracle just as convincingly (see Exodus 7).

There is a humorous episode in Acts where a secular glory-seeker tries to exorcise a demon in the names of Jesus and Paul. The demon—obviously schooled in one-liners—said, "Jesus I know, and Paul I know, but who are you?" (Acts 19:15 NKJV). Then the demon, far from being exorcised, jumped on the bogus miracle worker and beat him soundly.

Perhaps the missing humility we so long to see among evangelical miracle workers has evaporated as the office of "miracle worker" has grown by common consensus to be a special office given only to a few. To most Christians I know, it is inconceivable they could "do a healing." Somehow, it never occurs to them. Here and there I have known a mother with a sick child who took the child to a faith healer. It always strikes me as incongruous. They love their child more than any faith healer ever could. They love Christ as much as any faith healer ever could—in fact they often love Christ more altruistically, for they make no salary by "working" for Christ. They are inevitably far more humble, yet they often go to the richest and most arrogant of show-biz ministers to ask for healing.

Communion: The Birthplace of Power

There is little that inflames piety like a service of communion. What is there about bread, wine, and a focus on the cross that brings human need and God's supply together? We do not know for certain. But it does. So often when I have not felt my physical best, a communion service has the effect of healing. As a pastor, in taking communion to the hospital I have often perceived an immediate strength coming into the communicant just from receiving the bread, the word, and the wine.

In 1986, when my wife's grandfather was ninety-six, he fell and broke his hip. The doctor summoned his widely spread family from many states and we assembled to have "final prayers" with Grandpa. We did not serve communion, but we invoked the cross and asked God to grant Gramps a safe passage into heaven. Grandpa then asked to pray and he began to pray for all of us. His prayer swelled in fervor till they echoed down the corridors of the hospital. I told my wife, when we left the hospital, that Grandpa would not die—his exuberant prayers had convinced me he was healed. He actually lived to 102 years of age. It was a kind of "final communion" that was not so final—a moment of empowerment that bestowed healing upon a supposedly dying man. Many attest to these kinds of experiences.

In his marvelous confession *Memoirs of a Lunatic*, Leo Tolstoy said that his confused childhood came to focus in inner healing and salvation at communion. He says that all his wrongs were healed when he took the bread and wine: "Then the light fully illumined me and I became what I now am. If there is nothing of all that—then it certainly does not exist with me. And there at the church door I gave away to the beggars all I had with me—some thirty-five rubles—and went home on foot talking with the peasants."[37] If Tolstoy could so experience God and salvation, I certainly should not ignore its miraculous power.

Final communion (last rites) is one of the sacraments of the Catholic Church. There, where life is often to be measured in minutes, the priest brings the dying Christian to one last focus on the cross and the great sacrifice of the Savior. Is there a miracle here? Of course—the miracle of eternal life and of Calvary confidence soars. To affirm the true reality of heaven, by sipping of the body and blood, is to gain the complete confidence of heaven from the final vista. There, above the cup, looms heaven.

Many Christians see communion as the bookends of life. They celebrate both First Communion and Last Rites. Thus they place the cross on either end of their maturing years. The miracle here is that such temporary things as bread and wine should teach—at first communion—the saving glory of Christ and His cross. Then at last rites the cross wraps it all together once again.

Still, many feel formal liturgical churches have invested communion with too much power. In 1215 the Fourth Lateran council proclaimed officially the doctrine of transubstantiation—the belief that when the priest said, *"Hoc est corpum meus,"* the bread and wine were miraculously transformed into the body and blood of Christ. It does not appear that way, the council said, to keep it from becoming too repulsive to the communicants. But it is the actual body and blood of Christ. These churchmen appealed to John 6:53, where Jesus said, "Except you eat the flesh of the son of man and drink his blood you have no life in you (KJV)." Thus communion becomes the only way to have eternal life. Every mass then becomes a new and actual crucifixion where the dying Jesus is actually present when the priest intones the Latin words, *"Hoc est corpum meus."* These are sacred, miraculous words, but because the common people of that day did not understand Latin, *"hoc—us—est"* became *"Hocus Pocus,"* a phrase we still retain as words of magic. To earlier generations, this church magic became the great *abracadabra* that actually changed wine to blood. Thus to ordinary souls magic and miracles came together at communion, which changed the whole view of communion. If one accidentally dropped the bread and wine after it had been blessed, he became guilty of sacrilege for playing so loosely with the body of the crucified Christ. Thus, although the bread was given to the worshipper, the cup was not, out of fear the blood might be spilt and the blood of Christ desecrated.

Breakfast as a term came to be from such a lofty view of communion. Communicants fasted before communion so as not to "mix in their stomachs" the body and blood of Christ with ordinary foods. After communion was over they "broke fast" to eat their morning meal, hence the word *breakfast.*

But the power of communion became enlarged to include the right to go to heaven. The priest, according to John 6:53, held the power of eternal life. If he refused communion he damned the soul of those from whom the body and blood were withheld. Excommmunion or excommunication was not merely to keep people from taking communion, it was to damn them eternally to hell. Thus when the pope excommunicated Martin Luther (or in our own time Fidel Castro) it was a weighty and eternal matter.

How influential was the concept of eating and drinking the actual Christ? Kenneth Woodward (upon whose work I have leaned heavily for this book) said:

Now surprisingly, the Eucharist itself became productive of a wide variety of miracles as well as the subject of hymns like "Panis Angelicus," attributed to Saint Thomas Aquinas. "To eat God," as Caroline Walker Bynum has observed, "was to take into one's self the suffering flesh on the cross.

In the later Middle Ages, physical identification with Christ became even more literal. The mystic provided a new and powerful image of the saint and was more likely to be a woman than a man. Moreover, female mystics were more likely than male to experience stigmata, levitations of the body, and other physical manifestations associated with divine rapture.[38]

But this magical power of communion was stripped away by the reformers in the fifteenth century. Huldrych Zwingli, a contemporary of Luther's, said there was no real presence in the bread; all flesh, even the human flesh of Jesus, was worthless in its power to redeem. By the time Martin Luther died in 1546 all images, relics, and confidences in the magical transformation was gone. In its place, concurrent with the translation of the Bible into the common tongue, rose the preaching of the Word. While modern evangelicals go centrally to this preaching, both Catholics and Protestants agree on the importance of communion to the ongoing spiritual breath of the church.

What is the real miracle force in communion? The meal itself suggests that the world is coming together into oneness. German bombs during World War II devastated the Coventry Cathedral. But years later when the newly restored, neogothic cathedral was dedicated, it was consecrated under a new cross of nails (made from the nails of bombed village houses) and there under the cross, German and British Christians held a communion where these once ancient enemies could be made one in Christ. "At the foot" of the cross all ground is level. Communion is the great leveler. Its greatest miracle may be one of unity, ever pulling together the fractured body of Christ.

Ascetisism: The Force of Miracle

Agnes of God was at first a Broadway play and later a Jane Fonda movie. The play begins with a wistful nun who has just had a baby, but can recall nothing of the rapist-seducer who took advantage of her. Agnes the nun lived a separated life in which even sin held no interest to her. She belonged to God to such an extent that nothing else mattered. She loved Him and could not be violated in her soul no matter who took advantage of her body.

Do such wholly Christ-obedient souls actually exist?

When miracles occur, they are often wrought by men and women who live holy lives. Sinlessness and miracles just seem to go together—the reward of a holy life.

But driving too hard for the holy life can breed a bad pathology. The history of Christianity is replete with examples of people who tried to "mortify" their spirituality by doing bizarre things just to prove their spiritual lives grew best when they sat their physical lives at naught. Catherine of Sienna drank pus to prove that the physical life was nothing. Angela of Folign drank the water she used to wash lepers. Francis of Assisi actually kissed lepers. Simon Styletes spent his life atop a tall pole to keep himself unspotted from the lower sinful world beneath him. On and on goes the list of those who tried to demonstrate that their physical lives were not as dear to them as their quest to live the holy life.

Evangelicals may dismiss these examples as bizarre and beneath their own more reasonable paths to devotion. But before we get too smug (or disgusted) about the matter, we need to remember we are not entirely guilt free on the subject.

In Kingston, Georgia, in 1990 Arnold Loveless was fatally bitten by a rattlesnake during one of his church's worship services. Two days after his funeral the church held another such service in its simple rural sanctuary. An article in the *Atlanta Constitution* described that service in this manner:

> *The Rev. Carl Porter, the pastor, warned the three dozen people in the pews, "We've got some serpents up here. They'll bite you, and they will kill you. If you get one of them out that's between you and the Lord."*
>
> *But the first rousing song of the evening was only a few choruses old when Mr. Byron Crawford, 28, and Gene Sherbert, and other church member felt led to take up the snakes.*
>
> *As all others in the church stood, clapped and swayed, Mr. Crawford sang a gospel song, sounding like a young Elvis Presley, whom he vaguely resembles.*
>
> *"He's the God of Alabama. He's the God of Tennessee. He's the God right here in Georgia. He's the God for you and me," he sang, accompanied by electric guitars, cymbals, drums and tambourines.*
>
> *For about 15 minutes, verse after verse, he held the copperheads, sometimes raising them to face level.*
>
> *Mr. Sherbert, meanwhile, held a 2½ foot rattlesnake, much like the one that killed Mr. Loveless. At one point, he placed it writhing on the pulpit.*[39]

Snakes have actually long been a way for the faithful to demonstrate the level of their holiness. The Hebrews have a tale in which Hanina ben Dosa, a very holy, sinless rabbi of the first century, cast out evil on the basis of his own holy living. It happened that a terrible water snake was biting people and plunging them into great sickness:

> *It happened that a water-snake lived in a certain place which used to injure people. They came and told Rabbi Hanina ben Dosa. He said to them, "Show me its nest." They showed him its nest. He placed his heel over the opening of the nest and this snake came out and bit him; and the water-snake died. He put it on his shoulder, brought it into the school and addressed them, "See, my children, it is not the water-snake which kills; sin kills." From that time on they used to say, "Woe to the man who meets a water-snake and woe to the water-snake that meets rabbi Hanina ben Dosa."[40]*

The story may well be untrue, and it's definitely bizarre, but it does illustrate that ancients believed in the power of a holy life to work miracles. Remember, Satan in Christian symbolism is often portrayed as a serpent (See Genesis 3) or a dragon (See Revelation 12). Holiness in such imagery often becomes the Dragon Slayer.

But how are the demons to be exorcised from the human spirit? By the believer's willingness to die to all ambition. Paul mentions in Romans 6:11 we are to reckon ourselves to be dead to sin but alive in Christ. But how do we reckon ourselves to be dead in sin? By being crucified with Christ. It is this belief that led to doctrines of mortification—putting to death of all that honors the self or seeks our personal comfort. Through these acts of mortification believers seek to prove they do not honor or cherish temporal existence. They are willing at every moment to die to themselves that Christ might be all in all.

Along with these acts of mortification many who lived holy lives also worked many miracles. They didn't want the credit for these miracles, but they did want to be as holy as human ability could permit. As a result of their mortification, God worked unbelievable things through their lives.

Charlatans do tricks. Holy men and women perform miracles—or at least God performs great miracles through their holy, obedient lives. Catholics have their holy servants categorized and more importantly canonized. We Protestants and evangelicals have no such official lists of holy people. Yet we do honor those men and women of the faith who enrich our lives with unexplainable meaning. In my younger years as a pastor, we had an older woman in our church who had served for forty years as a missionary to South America. She took no interest in movies, television, novels, or entertainments. She lived as unto the Lord and her personal prayers for me became treasure. I found I was able to battle fatigue and spiritual depression just by remembering her holy life and power to heal brokenness in others through her daily desire to be holy as Christ was holy.

Malcom Muggeridge once spent some time among the monks in Nunraw, Scotland. He was amazed that these simple, holy men were able to live out a meaningful code of faith developed while living completely separate from the world. He was at first skeptical as to why anyone would choose such an isolated way of life. But he had not been among them long before he had to ask himself: "Do these who pay the price of 'being crucified with Christ' [Galatians 2:20 NIV] not make life possible for the rest of us?"

It is a fair question. Do not two or three holy souls keep the rest of the world safe and alive? Remember Abraham as he bargains with the angels for the existence of Sodom: "Will you destroy the evil with the good? Will you for the sake of ten righteous pardon the wicked of the whole city?" (Genesis 18:32). And to Jeremiah God said, "Run to and fro throughout the streets of Jerusalem and find one righteous man and I will pardon the whole city" (see Jeremiah 5:1).

Those who discipline themselves to live consecrated lives not only work specific smaller miracles, but through them God makes the human race possible. Out of their self-denial is the miracle of human continuance in the face of an all requiring God.

Service: The Temple of Miracles and Wonders

Service is the art of those who are committed to being the hands of Christ in a hurting world. Service and ministry in and of themselves are a kind of miracle. Most ministers I know have used these more ordinary routes to more ordinary miracles. Some years ago I led a prayer retreat for the brothers at the Crozier Monastery in Nebraska. The Croziers are not a large order and for me to do a prayer retreat was an experience in oxymoron. My own spiritual shallowness has long troubled me, and for me to try and create any insights on the subject of prayer for these monks was a case of bringing spiritual coals to Newcastle.

But the best part of this endeavor was my meeting Brother Marty, who became a life-long friend. We rarely saw each other but our letters and greetings flew back and forth from his monastery to my suburban parish. How rich his life has made my own. He gave his life to working with mentally handicapped children. Most of the children never had a philosophical understanding of who he was or why he was somehow in their midst. Yet there he was, always loving and serving those who could never speak his name. This was a miracle I could understand. It was not a miracle breathtaking enough to put on cable television. But it was a miracle which instructed me in my suburban church.

At that time our church was growing rapidly and within a couple of decades I had baptized 2,800 people. It was full of upper-class executives who served as my brothers and sisters. When challenged with Jesus, we all managed a kind of casseroles-and-softball kind of Christianity. But against our secularized faith, there stood Brother Marty, loving for years those who never learned to speak his name.

I have spent a lot of time in recent years with the Salvation Army. Why have I been so intrigued with these uniformed saints? It can only be that I have found in them a street Christianity that keeps Christ in the downtown areas of a city, curing souls that would never be reached by the far-flung beltway mega churches that sprawl in seas of asphalt surrounded by Lexus-driving believers.

I have tried to remind myself that the poor and derelict of America are no more special to God than the sophisticated Christians of suburbia. But it is no use. When I ask myself where Jesus would have served, the inner city always wins over the outer one.

How my admiration for the Salvation Army grows. The institution is a place of miracles, small and large. When I see their red shield I come to attention, for I have seen some of the miracles that have made them famous. I can never consider their work without remembering one of their converts giving me the best definition of miracles. Said the new Christian, "I do not know how Jesus changed water into wine, but in my case He did something more valuable: He changed beer into furniture." These are the miracles that make the world rich.

I have only spent a brief time in Calcutta but that visit in some ways changed my worldview forever. Everything about this city spoke of offense. Eighty percent of the world's cities have no sewer systems, and Calcutta may epitomize the filth of such urban destitution. I could not at first understand why Lederer and Burdick called it the *City of Joy*. But I had not been there long before miracles began exploding all about me. Mother Teresa's presence in the city could be seen in the miracle of a tall and dignified American Episcopal woman I saw carrying medicine to men in one of the Houses for the Dying. It was a miracle she was there—a miracle to herself and to those whose death she gave dignity. It was a miracle that I met her. A miracle that showed Christ was alive in the world.

I stayed in a cheap hotel across from the place where every morning a group of Methodists in a white van pulled up along the sidewalks and served huge thirty-gallon caldrons of hot rice to a Hindu parish. I can still picture these wonderful denim-missionaries clumping clots of life-saving rice onto banana leaves to feed lines of the starving. Do modern Methodists—or Episcopals or Presbyterians, etc.—work miracles? Count on it. The white van serves as a symbol that miracles come at the hands of those who serve. The miracles of life.

Conclusion

The best miracle I saw in Calcutta was realized through David, a Baptist friend of mine. Prompted by a suggestion from Mother Teresa, he began buying armloads of day-old bread for the insane who wander the streets of Calcutta at night. These gangs of mentally challenged have no institutions to which they can go. They live and die starving in the filthy streets of the City of Joy.

They wander mostly at night, when the hordes of street children are sleeping. Since there is no other time to minister, David the Baptist goes into the streets at night to dispense day-old bread to those he will never be able to convert to Christianity and who, for all David's long nights of effort, will never call his name.

He knows them only as needy brothers. They know him only as the bread man. But the miracle is this: when David sees these needy ones, he sees Jesus. When they see him, they see him as a Jesus whose name will not form itself except in the miracle of bread. When God sees both of them, he sees Jesus, too.

And anonymous miracles flow.

Yet they are not quite anonymous. God is writing up all such works in his *Book of Miracles* for our later reading when Christ and those who continue His work are united in the presence of a Holy God. And what a grand and glorious reading that will be.

CHAPTER SEVEN

Do Miracles Still Happen and What Difference Does it Make?

A belief in miracles is not a vacation from reason . . . Not only is it reasonable to believe that miracles can and do happen, it is unreasonable to think they cannot and do not occur.

PHILOSOPHY PROFESSOR RALPH A. McINERNY

Do miracles still happen today?

Terry Mocny was awakened by a police officer one night and told that his son Ed had just been in a severe car accident. The impact of the crash had crushed the first vertebrae in his neck and separated his skull from his spine. His doctors in Ann Arbor told Ed's family that injuries like this were almost always fatal. When not fatal they resulted in lifelong paralysis.

Sixty-four days after the crash, Ed Mocny left the hospital. He walked out on his own. There were virtually no lingering effects from his injury. "Miracles do happen," Ed said. "I'm living proof of that."[41]

Is this an unusual happening? Hardly. Miracles like this are commonplace throughout the church of Jesus Christ. There is an old Hassidic saying: "He who believes all these sayings is a fool but he who cannot believe them is a heretic."[42] The same may be said of miracles. Those who believe too easily are gullible but those who will not believe any of the miracles are not believers at all. Still, between faith and gullibility lies the difficult matter of interpretation.

More difficult than understanding miracles is the matter of understanding miracle workers. Miracles, we generally believe, are most often performed by "important" people. The power to accomplish them resides in some unseen force that arises from their lives. Through the ages this power or force has often been attributed to physical things rather than the persons themselves.

Remember the woman who was healed of an "issue of blood" in Luke's gospel? She seemed to believe she would be healed if only she could touch the hem of Jesus' garment. In other words, Jesus' ability to heal did not reside only in himself—or even in the woman's confidence in him. This power also resided in the very clothes he wore.

The mantle of Elijah is but another example of this transference of the power of miracles from the prophet to his cloak. The first thing Elisha did when he picked up the cloak of the former prophet was to "try out its powers" for himself. "Where now is the Lord God of Elijah," said Elisha. With that he struck the river Jordan and the cloak of Elijah that had always divided the river for the old prophet divided it once again for the younger (see 2 Kings 52:14).

This belief in the power of physical items continued through the use of relics. Relics are artifacts the saints once possessed—even parts of their dead bodies. After a saint died, it was generally felt that their bones, clothes, or body fragments still held the residual power to work miracles. Hence church altars were often consecrated by the implantation of some bone from a miracle worker's skeleton. Clerics and lay persons alike believed, even centuries later, that these bones could supply power to cure the sick or shield whole communities from the contagion of the Plague.

The Devil, it was generally agreed throughout the Middle Ages, was afraid of holy water. So well-meaning priests often used it in exorcisms. Too, wax amulets were often fashioned out of the stubs of old altar candles and used to ward off the devil; these wax moldings were also said to be effective against lightning, fire, drowning, and child-bed death. In 1589 Wales people still crossed themselves when they shut their windows at night, or when they left their flocks in the fields. It was common to say to anyone who had experienced any misfortune, "This would not have happened if you had crossed yourself today." Later, in 1591 a certain John Allen was said to be in possession of a limited quantity of Christ's blood. He sold this blood for twenty English pounds per drop and guaranteed it to be effective against any kind of bodily assault or sickness.[43]

Augustine in the fourth century at first objected to the notion that relics contained the power of miracle in them. He felt the original and real abilities of physical possessions had been perverted. But in 416 when the newly discovered bones of Stephen, the first Christian martyr, were brought to Augustine's home city of Hippo seventy cures were reported to have occurred in the first two years. After this, Augustine viewed them with more regard.

Relics soon obtained a kind of intrinsic power in any religious community lucky—or "blessed"—enough to possess them. This type of belief is still held today—witness the widespread regard in which the Shroud of Turin is held. I have even visited one famous church in Europe where the "jewel encrusted" skeleton

of St. Felip lay in a glass reliquary. Being an evangelical, this
skeleton seemed to me to be both ghoulish and gaudy, too ornate
a horror to display inside a church. Still, I could not help but
wonder how often the sick and dying had resorted to this skeleton to seek or claim a cure.

Gregory was elected pope in 590 C.E. and was a great believer
in the power of relics. One of the saints, Gregory—a prolific
writer himself—venerated was Libertinus, who revered Honoratus' great power of miracle so much he never went anywhere
without carrying one of the saints sandals. Gregory says that
Honoratus' sandals were capable of restoring the dead to life:

*There was Libertinus, a highly respected man. He had lived as a
disciple under Honoratus and received his training from him.
Libertinus had made it a practice never to go anywhere without
carrying on his person one of Honoratus' sandals . . . On his way
to Ravenna it happened that he met a woman carrying her dead
child in her arms. She looked at the man of God and, acting on the
impulse of her maternal love, seized his horse by the bridle. Then,
invoking the name of God, she solemnly declared, "You shall not
pass until you have brought my son back to life!" . . . Fear kept
him from attempting to fulfill a request so unusual, while a feeling
of compassion kept urging him to help the mother in her
bereavement. But thanks be to God, the pious mother was vic-
torious in this struggle, and the saint, in being overcome, gave
proof of real strength. For, if the devotion of the mother had not
been able to conquer his heart, how could he have been a man of
true virtue? So he dismounted, knelt down, and raised his hands to
heaven. Then, taking the sandal from the folds of his garment, he
placed it on the breast of the dead child and, as he continued
praying, the boy came back to life. Libertinus took him by the hand*

and gave him back to his weeping mother. After that he continued on his way to Ravenna."[44]

Of course relics themselves are more or less invalid without the fervent belief in and use of divine names. Names have always been used as channels of miracles and power. The name of YHWH has special covenant power in the Hebrew faith. *Jesus,* likewise, is a name of power. Many television healers use the phrase "in the name of Jesus" to call forth their special healing power. This is certainly true in the case of exorcisms. When driving out demons, exorcists demand in the name of Jesus that those demons leave their host. What power resides in the name!

Relics . . . divine names . . . How are we ever to interpret miracles unless we learn to believe in their possibility? Miracles assault our credibility. We are no more prone to believe than we are to doubt. Our interest in science and learning is no accident. Our very name, *homo sapiens,* means "knower." Our five senses have allowed us to gather and classify all phenomena: this surface is smooth and that is rough; this tastes sweet; that is acrid; she is lovely, he is homely. Listen to the viola and evensong; quit banging on the pipes! Thus we move through life using our senses to sample and categorize existence.

But we learn more easily than we trust. We are forever sticking our index finger on the white surfaces beneath "Wet Paint" signs. We will not believe without a sample of cool pigment on our finger. If our finger comes up dry, we will lay our hand on the wall, and if necessary push and rub the defiant surface to make it yield a smudge.

Touching wet walls is the Adam in us. We are incurable believers, yet paradoxically incurable unbelievers. Adam had only one

"Wet Paint" sign in Eden. The sign clearly said "Bad Apples!" Adam must have leaned against the sign for days, fondling the fruits and asking himself, "Is it or not?"

Adam was created to live forever. Forever may not be a category you understand till you don't have it anymore. Still he must have wondered just how long a man could live without testing the truth of the sign. The fever to know raged. Had the Lord God posted the sign only to drive him mad with the lust to know? Desire welled up and consumed him. Satan tempted Adam with the taunt that there was yet one thing he didn't know—the tactile feel of the forbidden, the sensuous delight of paint on the finger.

Adam may have led the entire race into doubt, but he has not kept us there. We gather data for ourselves beneath the signs of our existence. There are none who never doubt. Some doubt all and are called atheists. Some doubt most and are called agnostics. Some doubt only a little and are called believers.[45]

UFOs and The Like

What exactly does it mean to be a believer? It means that the original hunger of Adam—the drive to know by experience—has been abridged. Believers can lay aside their need to prove the paint is wet; they have said to those rubbing the walls that they are willing to trust the sign. Miracles lie at the point of faith where we are unable to gather data. We are liberated to believe what is beyond our understanding.

As I mentioned earlier, many cultural surveys in the West have indicated that 90 percent of Westerners believe in God and fully 82 percent believe that miracles still happen today. However most Americans are Protestants and Protestants have been traditionally very skeptical of miracles. Protestant skepticism is rooted in their Reformation, where the reformed were all too eager to shuck the naïve trappings of the illiterate churchmen of the Middle Ages and put all miracles back into the Bible rather than in their living, breathing world. So the reformers, while honoring the miracles of Scripture, denied the contemporary miracles of their day. Most of them went so far as to say that all miracle-working ceased with the death of the apostles. More recently, Rudolf Bultmann went so far as to say it was impossible for modern Christians to believe in the New Testament world of miracles.[46]

Post-moderns are far more generous with their credulity. Still, the glitzy miracles of cable television make you wonder. Miracles, like most things that challenge our senses, have to be examined at arm's length.

Some years ago, UFO reports were coming in rather quickly. Flying saucers were landing here and there across the country, alarming observers—which seemed to me the objects' only real function. One report came in that particularly angered me as an unbeliever in UFOs: a man in my hometown saw a flying saucer at a prominent intersection that I crossed nearly every day. After his encounter with the alien spacecraft, he was visibly shaken. My wife read me the newspaper article describing how this poor, hysterical man had to be taken to a local hospital.

"What do you think he saw?" my wife asked.

"Nothing," I said with a great deal of irritation. "Have you noticed how everybody sees UFOs but no one ever takes a picture? Do you know why nobody takes a picture?"

My wife could see I was becoming angry.

"No," she said simply. "Do you know why?"

"Because it's hard to photograph schizophrenia."

A few days later just at dusk we were going to the market only a block or so from our home. As we came to a stop sign I suddenly caught sight of some little saucer-shaped blips of light undulating in the sky just above the horizon. I studied the sky and said to my wife, "Oh, look! What are those things?"

"Do you know what they look like?" she asked. We both knew what they looked like. I squinted as she dryly asked, "Okay, smart aleck, where's your camera?"

There clearly was something there; it was the interpretation of the phenomenon that was the problem. In this instance my own viewpoint was clouded by unbelief. Once I had stamped my foot on the floor and said there were no flying saucers, only intellectual repentance could make change possible. I still don't know what we saw that day.

All this is to say the interpretation of unreasonable phenomena, including miracles, has never been easy.

Do Miracles Happen Today?

Deepak Chopra has become famous as the Eastern guru on spiritual healing. Author Douglas Connelly had this to say about him:

He at first made the transition from a leader in the Transcendental Meditation movement to the head of the mind-body medicine division of a prestigious southern California hospital . . . What Chopra actually promotes are ancient Hindu principles known as Ayurveda. According to these principles, miracles of healing do not come from the hand of God but are examples of "the spontaneous remission of disease." New Age healing techniques are closer to magic than to miracle. Chopra has become nothing more than a pagan shaman to a sophisticated secular society that desperately seeks some way to overcome the relentless drumbeat of the aging process. [47]

The shelves of secular bookstores abound with books by psychic "healers" and astrologists full of such advice for their confused patrons. Astrology is always a first step into the need for information and those hungry for its "insights" flock to their star-chart gurus for help. This affliction is old; it was a constant concern of the Old Testament prophets. Throughout the Middle Ages it survived as powerfully as it does today. By the reign of Elizabeth I astrology was commonplace in England. It was customary for medieval kings to consult with astrologers to figure out how to best govern their people. In 1649, it is documented, the Marquis of Huntley lamented that he believed the stars and they deceived him. [48]

Not only contemporary astrologers but also contemporary psychics foster a wide-spread belief in miracles. Chopra's vast popularity points to a cultures-wide interest in contemporary miracles—although not a belief in the true meaning and source behind them.

As I mentioned earlier, I grew up in Enid, Oklahoma, where it seemed to me no miracles ever happened. Yet I must confess that even my little Baptist world was filled with great believers in miracles. I remember when my brother died at age ten there was much talk of heaven, and those souls around me spoke of the place as eagerly and realistically as we spoke of Garfield County where we lived. My brother would be back with us in the Resurrection, they said. It seemed to my grieving family be the greatest of all miracles.

In my childhood, the Baptists I knew counted on concrete miracles like the Resurrection. But I remember a time when a farmer near Bison, Oklahoma, said that the Virgin Mary had appeared to him. Even at that age my credulity was challenged. Mary had come to Garfield County—she hardly ever did—and we were all amazed. I remember asking my mother what she was doing there in Garfield County, barely eleven miles from our home, but Mother had no idea. There is still a granite stone just off US Highway 81 marking the place where Mary showed up.

Of course we Baptists were not as big on the Virgin's appearance as local Catholics. We would have been more impressed if John the Baptist had showed up. Still from that time on I found myself intrigued by all the Virgin Mary seemed to get done, what with her incessant miracles and her heavy schedule of personal appearances. I remember reading in the paper that a stone Virgin was crying in Oaxaca, Mexico. I asked Mother why a stone Virgin would cry. But Mother, who'd had no answer as to the Virgin's appearance in Bison, Oklahoma, was once again skeptical.

Then in 1975 Mrs. Anne Poore of Philadelphia said that her statue of Jesus had begun to bleed real drops of blood from his wounded hands. I remember thinking how much better it seemed to me for Jesus to get the publicity. Still, the bleeding statue wakened in me a strong protest of reason.

All of this causes me to realize that miracles require interpretation. My mother, who firmly believed my little brother would be back again at the great resurrection, was instantly skeptical of a stone Virgin crying in Mexico. Why?

Several issues of interpretation began to occur to me.

Miracles that happen further back in time seem more credible than miracles that happen now.

"Now" miracles never seem as credible as ancient ones. A miracle in 1990 is somehow less believable than one that occurs in 1590.

But Augustine, who lived in the fourth century, felt the same way about first-century miracles:

> *As a young theologian, the great church father Augustine (354–430) believed that miracles were necessary in Jesus' day to persuade people that Jesus was the Messiah. Miracles ended with the Apostles, he said, so that believers would not seek merely visible assurance for their faith and because miracles, by becoming customary, would no longer be wondrous. Later in life Augustine clarified his position and said that he did not mean that no miracles would occur but that they would be fewer and less public than Jesus' miracles. As a faithful pastor to the Christians in Hippo, a city in Roman North Africa, Augustine had seen many miracles that God had given to comfort and encourage his people.*[49]

I suppose for all of us it is just harder to believe God could really work now like He used to (or perhaps that He'd want to!). For example, most of us are more prone to believe in the miracle of Dunkirk than we are to believe in the miracle of Bosnia. Earlier in the book I referred to the American pilot who found himself crash landing in Bosnia. In a harrowing tale of survival he made his way out of enemy territory into safety. He gave the credit for his miraculous odyssey to the Virgin Mary, whose recent visits to Medjugorje seemed to lend some credibility to his tale. Yet this "miracle" is too recent to have the widespread acceptance of a miracle performed in the Middle Ages.

Rasputin, the Russian merchant monk who gained such stature in the court of Nicholas and Alexandra, became the great saint of the Romanovs for keeping their hemophilic son Alexis alive. Yet most (nearly everyone except the Romanovs) saw Rasputin as an opportunist and trickster. On the other hand, most of us who now doubt Rasputin greet the apostolic miracles of the Book of Acts with immediate acceptance. I began this chapter relating a story about the handling of snakes. These days, snake handling is an accepted form of worship for some rural Appalachian churches. Yet, for most of us, singing "The Old Rugged Cross" while we pass a diamondback down the pew seems unworthy of the word *miracle*. To those of us who doubt, most snake handlers who come home from the church unbitten seem more lucky than blessed. But being a fan of Madame Guyon, who triumphed over poisonous snakes, I am prone to believe that she encountered a snake in triumph and with one godly rebuke ordered the serpent from the path. Why? Maybe because it happened in another century and time. It just seems more likely to have happened.

Miracles that happen farther away seem more likely than those that happen in our neighborhood.

For some reason we all seem to distrust the miracles that happen close to us. Perhaps it's just that it's hard to imagine someone down the street or in the next town having a supernatural experience. After all, if we haven't had them, why would someone else? Therefore, the local farmer we all know who saw the Virgin Mary in Bison, Oklahoma, seems less to be trusted than those who saw the Virgin Mary in Mejugorje, Bosnia.

Even the most outstanding encounter with miracle that we in Enid ever felt was the focus of evangelical skepticism, when Oral Roberts began his faith-healing crusade in the Enid Convention Center. Oral had, while in high school, contracted tuberculosis and had hemorrhaged for 163 straight days before his father came to him praying for him to be "saved." Oral gave his life to

Christ but was not immediately healed of TB. This came later when Oral went to a faith healer who shouted over Oral, demanding of what he called the demonic sickness, "You foul sickness! Come out of this boy." Thus came Roberts' healing and his own call to heal others.

The point is that when Roberts began his miracle working in Enid it caused a considerable stir. Most did not look upon his efforts with encouragement. They doubted rather than opened their eyes to the possibility, and thus lost their opportunity to exalt in a miracle, should it happen. I remember a story about a blind girl who had a candy concession in the courthouse. Roberts, it was said by many, was unable to heal her blindness because she refused to exhibit faith that he could heal her. He had apparently asked the girl to send her "seeing-eye" dog home as a testament to belief that Oral could heal her. Alas, she did not do as Oral asked, and after the miracle crusade was over she remained blind. The inference was that if she really believed that she could be healed, she would have trusted God enough to send her dog home.

Catholics seem more believable than do Protestants when they talk about miracles.

When I stood at the Shrine of Guadalupe watching rural pilgrims lost in rapturous, miracle-seeking prayer, I felt inspired, as though the shrine might actually be working miracles for some of these simple believers. Likewise, the chapel of Chimayo not far from our New Mexico home seems a better representation of a miracle-dependent community than the little Pentecostal chapels of my childhood. This Chimayo church has had pilgrims coming by the thousands in search of cures for themselves or a loved one. The place is filled with *milagros*—little pewter or silver amulets of things like legs, hands, heads. Kissing them, the pilgrims laid them on the altar as they waited for their own legs, hands, or heads to be cured. I've never seen anyone at Chimayo actually cured, but it seems like a more apt place to get the job done than a cable telecast might be. And more important, those pilgrims come believing in the power of miracles.

It probably seems to Protestants and evangelicals (whether or not the actual miracle rates differ) that Catholics get more miracle mileage out of their shrines than evangelicals get out of their telecasts or tent meetings. The miracles that do occur around us today are often—to our minds—poorly authenticated and therefore less believable to us skeptics. In the case of my childhood in rural Oklahoma, it was the odd procession of itinerant miracle evangelists that became the focus of our doubt. One set of brothers I will never forget wore sequined jackets, and denounced the demons of five-card stud, canasta, and the tango. They also worked "miracles." Of course, like most of the dedicated souls I knew, I had never learned to play cards, dance, or go to movies. But whatever we believed about movies or drinking, we were interested—in a passive sort of way—in the miracles of which they spoke but could never prove. These two brothers appeared to be very godly and most fanatically devoted to God. One brother said he had once been dead for forty-eight hours before the other brother raised him to life again. He had spent those "48 hours in Hell"—the title of his revival tract. As I watched them, I wondered why the one brother had raised the other—the main preacher of the dynamic duo—to life. It could not have been in the interest of sermon excellence. And so we went away unconvinced.

Conversely, when we hear of Catholic miracles, we are immediately fascinated and more apt to believe. One remarkable

Catholic phenomenon is the Stigmata. In the year 1224 Francis of Assisi longed to be crucified with Christ. He had always wanted to die as a martyr for Christ, but that possibility became inaccessible to him. But to his way of thinking God had given him identity with Christ—he experienced the Stigmata, through which by his own will he achieved this martyrdom. Frances did not flaunt his devotion but tried to hide his God-given wounds, forbidding others to speak of them or praise him for having them.

Saint Bonaventure in writing his biography of Francis said:

Francis now hung, body and soul, upon a Cross with Christ; he burned for love for God worthy of a seraph and like Christ he thirsted for the salvation of the greatest possible number of human beings. In other words, the grace of the stigmata was divine confirmation of the life he had chosen to live—and of what most Christians already believed him to be: he was not just another living saint but, as much as any human being could be, an alter Christus, a second Christ.50

Padre Pio was also given the gift of the Stigmata. His identity with Christ was all the more evident, though like Francis he refused to acknowledge his miracles, or gloat over his Stigmata. He was beatified in 1999 by the Pope and canonized in 2002, a mere thirty years after his death.

Of course, the big difference between Protestant miracles and Catholic ones is this: the Catholic Church requires every "official" miracle to pass beneath the acid test of its scrutiny. Every reported miracle is checked out and "verified" before any miracle worker is granted the right to claim it.

One can only wonder how American cable-television miracles would stand up to such scrutiny.

Conclusion

Saul of Tarsus once smirked over superstitious Christians who believed in the Resurrection. He no doubt thanked God that he had been to the Jewish seminary and recognized primitive religion when he saw it. Then all of a sudden he was confronted by the desert savior and found himself asking, "Who is it?" Had my wife been there she would have said, "Okay, seminary grad, where's your camera?" Paul had to deal with a phenomenon he had already decided not to believe in. And when the Christ of the Damascus Road said, "I am Jesus," Paul did not have the audacity to say, "But you're in the graveyard; I've been telling everyone."

We need to be equally as accepting. There can be no doubt these days that there yet seems to be an ample number of healings and natural miracles. It is only logical to assume, therefore, that the age of miracles is not past. Credibility must be given to all kinds of claims, from cable television to Lourdes to Medjugorje. The stigmata, relics, the Shroud of Turin, healings, etc., must all be summoned forth to help convince us miracles are no less likely in this moment than they were in the era of the Caesars. Further, the world cannot live without the wonder of all that God can do in outperforming its understanding, for a world without belief is a stagnant world.

Of course, once you begin to search for contemporary miracles, you are soon to discover that for every authentic one you find, you must deal with some that smack of trickery. Miracles and tricks have always passed closely. Yes, it is easy to believe that Jesus fed the five thousand. But then, you also have to reckon with a sincere woman frying her tortillas in New Mexico. The miracle may lack the grandeur of the Resurrection, but that does not mean it didn't happen.

The children of Fatima, Portugal, saw the Virgin, they said, and she gave them letters to be opened on the assigned future dates. Do you believe? Millions have now made pilgrimages to the cathedral that marks the spot of the miracle. You have but to mention single geographical names to summon up volumes of miraculous claims: Lourdes, Medjugorje, Guadalupe, Fatima, Turin. And yet, note these places and events are the domain of the Catholics. Remember, the rare Oklahoma appearance of the Virgin made all the Baptists angry. Mary has never attracted many admirers in solidly evangelical areas, so Mary's Bible-belt appearances rarely get anywhere.

The Catholics confidently belive in miracles. We evangelicals must learn to do the same. God is still alive and doing unexplainable and glorious things in the lives of those who believe. As Jesus told us, all things are possible . . .

CHAPTER EIGHT

Exorcisms: Christ's Most Important Miracles

Spiritual warfare is just as brutal as human warfare.
RIMBAUD

Jesus' encounter with and defeat of Satan was the center of His earthly struggle. Exorcisms therefore dominate Christ's earthly sojourn. Why are these miracles so important? They lie at the heart of Christ's cosmic, invisible struggle. Had He been unable to defeat Satan in these miracles, His eventual struggle with Satan in the garden of Gethsemane would have been unwinnable. The cross would have been of no lasting significance. To some degree the whole doctrine of Christ's sinlessness focuses on how He won over every battle with evil.

Exorcisms: The Work of Embodied Holiness

Chris Kline, a host for a Christian radio station in Virginia, has experienced the deceptive power of demons firsthand. As a young woman she pursued a lifestyle centered on drugs, immorality, and drunkenness. On May 13, 1974, in the grip of an alcohol- and drug-induced high, Chris heard a voice in her room: "Don't be afraid, Chris. I am God, and I have a message for you." A brilliant white light filled her head and flooded her being with peace. The "voice" now resided in her. What followed were months of instructions from this new inner voice, volumes of automatic writing (more than four thousand pages), and her personal belief that God was trying to get her to produce a book that would convey His message to the world. But the self-destructive, sinful lifestyle continued.

Finally, after ten years under what she eventually realized was Satan's power, Chris trusted Christ as her Savior. Over the following months she was set free from the bondage she had known for so long. Looking back, Chris Kline believes that she opened herself to demonic oppression through her lifestyle and that she was controlled by a demon pretending to be the inner voice of God. Her testimony is powerful: "Evil spirits tried to destroy me; they came very close to succeeding. Satan came to me as 'an angel of light' but instead of giving me the freedom I wanted, he entangled me slowly but surely in his cords of death."[51]

Chris's casting of Satan from her life lacks the drama and glitz some contemporary exorcists might have shown in casting the demon out. But this raises the question of how Christ's ancient exorcisms compare with those done by contemporary healers. Those who are best at exorcisms have always been those with a high quotient of humble holiness. There is much truth in old adage: "The devil trembles when he sees the weakest saint upon his knees." Demons are best driven from the possessed by men and women with an unflagging commitment to God, for the power to exorcise derives from a focused obedience to Christ. Demons have no desire to enter into conflict with a holy life.

Earlier I referred to Saint Anthony, who was born around 250 C.E. and died in 356. His amazing life spanned 106 years and it was a life wholly given to rigorous asceticism and holy living. Throughout his years he wrestled with demons. It was said that when any poor, possessed person was brought into his presence, the demons fled their captive, for they could not live in the presence of such utter holiness as possessed Anthony's life.

One young demoniac was brought to Anthony in such a hideous state he devoured his own excrement. Anthony was moved to deep pity and stayed up all night praying that the young man might be free of the demon. At the break of day the demoniac jumped on Anthony, knocking him about. Those who had brought the young man in for healing grew angry with the man for his rough treatment of the saint. Anthony said: "Do not be angry with the young man, for he is not responsible, but the demon in him. And because of his censure and his banishment to arid places, he raged and he did this. So glorify the Lord, for in this way his assault on me has become a sign of the demon's departure." After Anthony spoke these words the young man was well. He suddenly knew where he was. He then embraced the old man, all the while giving thanks to God.[52]

But in spite of his remarkable exorcisms Anthony was most insistent that all of the glory for exorcism should be given totally to Christ. As author Kenneth Woodward wrote, "We ought not to boast about expelling demons, or become proud on account of healings performed . . . For the performance of signs does not belong to us—this is the Savior's work."[53]

In studying the life of Christ we see that demons always quaked before His holiness. Who may serve as an exorcist? Anyone who feels pity for the oppressed and at the same time understands that every attempt at helping people to be free must come from a committed life, schooled in the discipline of prayer. At the same time we must not turn our compassion from those who suffer under the control of the evil one merely because we feel we have not the spiritual excellence to stand against Satan.

I remember years ago a poor college freshman who became severely spastic in a meeting where I was the visiting preacher. I found myself at first puzzled as to the boy's condition. I do not generally leap to conclusions, and I was not eager to believe that the young man was a demoniac. But when I had at last determined he was not afflicted with epilepsy or some other explainable malady, I labeled the situation for what it was.

Then I encountered a greater fear within myself. Did I have the kind of holy living that would enable me to perform an exorcism? The answer I felt was "No." Still, the poor boy was so totally at the mercy of Satan I felt I had no choice but to try and exorcise the demon, so I did try.

Suddenly and at once the demon left and the boy knew peace. I was in awe at the power of Christ. *Non Nobis Domine*—*"Not to us, Lord"*—came to me. Like Anthony I saw myself as most unworthy. Christ alone was Savior and healer here.

I believe that the charge of healing of all who are so oppressed belongs to the body of Christ as a whole. However, we should all be reluctant to call ourselves exorcists; it is better to let such healing occur within the community and then give the community—or God—credit for the healing. After all, as Anthony reminds us, "It is all the work of Christ" anyway.

Whenever I write on this subject I ask myself if I am not being too cock-sure about a deeply spiritual issue. Yet ordinary Christians do have their part to play in the work of God.

Psychologist Scott Peck in his brilliant *People of the Lie* views exorcism as the most reasonable of all possible courses at the time. Yet he does not approach the task with the same humility of spirit one sees in Anthony. He calls these dark souls ever susceptible to Satan as "People of the Lie." Peck describes the intense satanic nature of those who allow an invasion of evil to control them. He tells, for instance, of a teenager who committed suicide with a rifle, and how the boy's evil-possessed father then gave his surviving son that very rifle the next Christmas. The boy who received the rifle in time became one of Peck's clients. When he came to Peck for treatment, his face was crusted with scabs, psychological evidence that the boy was trying to destroy himself (by picking holes in his skin). Scott Peck offers this case as evidence of extreme evil. Satan—while he does not possess all such souls—was responsible for the evil that was destroying that young man.

It is rare that a psychologist speaks so openly about exorcisms, for exorcisms are not a method of dealing with bad psychology but with demon possession. Real exorcisms are most possible when the Christ who owns the exorcist is allowed to confront and defeat Satan out of a devout life of holiness.

There are several categories of demons. Each of these must be explored in terms of how Jesus confronted the other kingdom and wins. For instance, there seem to be demons whose major purpose is to blaspheme God. There seem to be demons whose major purpose is to destroy people's minds. There are other demons that war against health and happiness.

But first let's understand Jesus' viewpoint on demons. Jesus saw all of Satan's realm as another kingdom. This other kingdom is a kingdom of darkness. It is as real as the kingdom of light but not as enduring. This realm has already been judged and is in the process of passing away. The moment Satan sought "to exalt his throne above the stars" (Isaiah 14:13), he was judged and his judgment is sure. He has come down to the earth "furious in his descent," but he knows that his time is short. Jesus will ultimately wipe his presence from the cosmos and the heavenlies. In the meantime Jesus confronts him, soul by soul, demon by demon, and drives him from the lives he wishes to destroy.

Categories of Demonic Conflict

Psychology has taught us to rename the demons in an attempt to eliminate them from the world (although for the time being their presence persists) because exorcism is still the most logical and fruitful way to deal with what may appear to be a psychosis. We must be careful that we do not overdo this tendency to name all mental problems as demon possessions, yet we must admit that wherever minds and hearts suffer internally, a soul may need to be liberated from some dark obsession. Such inward destructive evil may not be demons, but all such mental hurt is demonic, in the best sense of the word.

All through Jesus' ministry, only six exorcisms are described in detail. Every one was a distinct kind of skirmish in a spiritual war. And while these demons are not categorized as such in the New Testament, their exorcisms do illustrate five distinct types.

The Demon of Sacrilege

The first is the sacrilege demon. Christian demonology does not assign a name to this evil spirit, but the Hindus call him the Asura demon. He dares to confront the omnipotence of God. In a sense, his behavior is described in classic form in the Book of Job as Satan arrogantly struts into the court of heaven. In 2 Baruch 29:4 (in the Apocrypha) this spirit of antitruth is pictured as the spirit of the great leviathan, the evil monster of chaos. He is the spirit of evil that reared its head against God (see Isaiah 14:12–21). He goes brazenly to church and disrupts worship with slanderous irreverence. In Mark 1:21–28 this demon disrupts the synagogue by wailing in terror.

William Peter Blatty's novel *The Exorcist* describes the Asura demon. Obscenities to the Lord and confrontation and challenge to God are his methods. He seems to be a kamikaze, knowing that his direct challenge to God is suicidal. Nonetheless, he goes through with it. He is the prototype of all other demons, brilliant in venom and sacrilege.

The Demon of Antimatter

The next type of demon, the antimatter demon, also has no name among Christians. But the Hindus call him the Rakshasa demon. It is the Rakshasa that corresponds to Satan in the Revelation of St. John. His name in the Apocalypse is Apollyon or Abaddon— the Destroyer (see Revelation 9:11).

The name *Destroyer* indicates Satan's feeling about matter. Remember, all matter exists because of the creation of God. If you wish to hurt a creative person, you cannot do it more effectively than to smash what he or she has made. If you are angry with a porcelain artist and want to strike him with vengeance, just enter his studio and pull his figurines from their shelves. As they shatter on the floor the artist dies within.

Some years ago in the Vatican I stood before Michelangelo's great Pietà, a marvel of form and grace. I thought of the artist, working alone, absorbed in his creation, hitting the chisel in tender sanctity. Somberness and shame came over me. The artist's labor had liberated the mother of our Lord from the stony captivity of her bereavement. Since 1499 she has sat there in sorrow holding her executed son. The artist had cut from angled stone the deepest reverence of his soul.

But some years ago, an assailant came. An Apollyon leapt the barrier with his hammer and defaced the great masterpiece. He knocked a chip from Mary's knee, and marred the artist's work. This is how the spirit of Rakshasa feels about the work of God. Smash it, mar it, deface it; write graffiti across the finished calligraphy of the universe!

Satan seeks to destroy more than the physical. There are two exorcisms of mute demoniacs (see Matthew 9:32–34; 12:22). Satan resented the creation of speech as he did the rest of God's works. And so came the Rakshasa! He smashes the motor coordination, shuts up the larynx, and curses the tongue. And the work of God is smashed. Man, created to speak, is silenced.

The Demon of the Graveyard

The third category of demons, defined by the church during the Middle Ages, was called the Boggart or graveyard demon. (A derivative of the word *Boggart* has survived in the word *bogeyman*.) Originally Boggarts were the psychopathic demons. Legion turned the man of the Gerasenes into an unmanageable monster who broke chains (see Luke 8:29). So he lived among the tombs as the village madman.

But the Gerasene's curse was loneliness. Ripped from society and stuck in a tombyard, immense storms of evil ripped his heart. He wanted love but the alien beings that crowded his life would not permit him the luxury of friends. They devoured his mind.

Graveyards are a testament to the separation of life and death. The Boggart reminds us that hell—ultimate separation—is the final state of those who refuse Christ on earth. Though we are communal beings, we are shut up in the walls of torment, isolated by pain. Those dying outside of Christ often find solace in saying they will not be the only ones in hell. But when we are separated from life, we find no crowds. Torment closes us in to ourselves. Friends do not exist.

The Demon of Sexual Depravity

The Incubus is the fourth kind of demon. Superstitious church leaders of the Middle Ages classified this as the demon of sexual distortion. We find no clear evidence of this demon in Jesus' teaching. But medieval commentators said the inner nature of the Incubus was characterized by same lust that lured the fallen angels from the rim of glory to seduce the earth women in Genesis 6:1–2. Although Jesus taught that angels were not permitted marriage (see Matthew 22:30), in 1 Corinthians 11:10 Paul may be suggesting that angels have some sexuality.

Whether or not the Incubus has any validity as a sexual being, we may be confident that sexuality, as a creation of God, is a target. Throughout Christianity, illicit sex has been a slur on the dignity of true faith from witches' covens to politicians. In our day, Satan has already defaced biblical sexuality to the point that it has little respect in our suave, modern culture.

The Demon of Mischief

The fifth and final demon is the Imp or demon of mischief. The boy of Matthew 17:14, described as an epileptic, suffered under the trickery of an inner foe. Sometimes the child fell into the water or fire. Always it looked like an accident, but always it was the result of the demon who threw him into such circumstances. This is characteristic of demonic Imps.

The destructive tendencies of the Imp closely resemble those of the Rakshasa, the antimatter demon. This should not surprise us since the continuing goal of Satan is to destroy all that God made.

These categories are, of course, too rigid. Demons are hard to identify. In Matthew 17, the disciples had some trouble curing the epileptic boy because they did not know whether they were really pursuing epilepsy or an Imp. And in possible contradiction to the categories I mentioned above, Luke 8:2 says Mary Magdalene once had seven devils—though some theologians suggest Jesus' use of the term *seven devils* is symbolic, identifying Mary as an adulteress who violated the seventh commandment. But my hope is that this discussion will help us better understand how demons affect those whom they inhabit. The most important thing is that healthy faith retains a belief in the demonic realm. Satan stands opposite God (although he is not an equal or an opposite dark force in the universe; Satan's power only appears great when he brings it against the weakness of human will). Skepticism is the enemy of both God and Satan. No one does God service who disbelieves in Satan. And those who disbelieve in personified evil soon cease to believe in personified good as well. Here is the weakness of some contemporary theology. When Satan is dismissed, God becomes elusive.

Exorcisms foreshadow the final victory of God over Satan. Ultimately the universe will be swept clean of evil's horrible reality. God will take the key to the great pit and call Leviathan into it forever. God and Adam will walk together once more in the cool of the day. The tree of the knowledge of good and evil will have its roots exposed, and the new Eden will never know the slithering of serpents.[54]

Pork Therapy at the Bay of Pigs

Demons apparently don't like hell very much. Who would? Their distaste for the abyss became obvious in Luke 8 when Legion's demons begged Jesus not to send them back to the pit of hell. They suggested that Jesus give them permission to enter into a herd of pigs. Why pigs? Sure, pigs did not hold much honor in Jewish theology. Still, the answer that ensues doesn't support any antikosher bias that Jesus might have had. I think Jesus is not so antipork as He is pro mental health.

However, pigs aside, this is the only place in the New Testament that Jesus appears to make a "side deal" with demons (Luke 8:31). He wasn't being kind to the demons or forgetting all that demons stand for. He allowed the demons to go into pigs, and then the pigs ran down the embankment and were buried in the cold waters of the Sea of Galilee. Why did Jesus get into all this "swiney spirituality"? Why was He so kind to the demons?

Mostly likely because the fleeing, insane pigs were a powerful witness of healing to Legion. It must have been a clear sign to the demoniac that the demons which controlled him were gone. Jesus allowing the demons their request was a kind of "pork therapy" that must have been utterly convincing to the demoniac. Jesus was not trying to be kind to the demons, but to the demoniac.

These are the footprints of grace. Legion was insane, unkempt, naked, wild, and he smelled bad. But there is no hiding from

God's love. Jesus comes even into the graveyard to rout out the unclaimed.

See them! Jesus and the demoniac. They rush together and he raises his fierce hands as though he will crush Jesus' skull. Ah, but Christ, his lover, catches his fearful, trembling soul and smiles into those wild eyes, and orders out the demons. Then presto! The man sitting with Jesus is clothed and in his right mind.

I am big on irresistible grace. I don't understand it, but it seems to me for reasons of His own, Jesus sometimes breaks upon our existence and rebukes our demons and we find ourselves sitting with Him clothed and in our right minds. And only the reeking pile of pigs at the bottom of the precipice remind us how far His miracles extend to teach us that His healing is complete.

Continuing with this story, notice that in Luke 8:29 a single demon is mentioned, but for the next four verses it speaks of demons in the plural. It is like the film *The Three Faces of Eve*. There are multiple personalities from the Abyss. The demoniac was so filled with the powers of hell, he had lost all track of who he was.

This is the high and wicked crime of demons. They steal human identity. And Christ gives it back, as simple as that. That is the miracle of exorcism. We never own our souls until Jesus rescues them for us and we them give them back unto Him. And are born anew. It is an amazing thing.

Look at demonaic, that shaggy, naked giant. Called from a graveyard, sitting with Christ above the bay of pigs, he called for a robe and looked into the eyes of Christ, saying, as it were, "Praise the Lord, I am born again!" And being born again he took upon himself a glorious robe of decency. So the demons fled into pigs and the pigs were choked in the sea.

Does it seem far too radical? Does it seem more respected to stick with those user-friendly megachurch manuals? Is it more spiritual and chic to work on our drama clubs and Christian rock combos? Healing those with demonic-damaged identities takes courage. A courage to live in the graveyards. There just aren't enough pigs to heal a culture anyway.

Exorcism: Helping the World to Health

The Scott Peck book I earlier referred to contains a refreshing look at exorcism in terms of mental health. So many mental difficulties of our day were referred to in Jesus' day as "demon possession." Schizophrenia, psychosis, multiple personalities—even epilepsy—in Christ's day were seen to be the result of demonic depression.

Following the 1974 film version of William Peter Blatty's novel *The Exorcist*, there arose a flurry of mental health problems across America. I was a pastor in the suburbs during those days and the novel and movie caused widespread manias to surface. One night around 2:00 A.M., one of my members called me in a state of hysteria. Her mood was so agitated, I could understand only every other word or so. But I understood enough to put her wild conversation together. She was screaming that Mimi, her three-year-old, was possessed of a demon. The girl's possession, she said, was just like the "girl's in that demon movie." I knew "that demon movie" was *The Exorcist*. I assured her I would be right over, and as soon as I had dressed I made my nocturnal way across the city to her house.

When I got there, I saw a very frightened three-year-old cowering in a corner of the master bedroom. Her mother, who had just called me, was still hysterical as her husband tried to calm her down. As I entered the room, the mother was screaming and pointing to her child, saying she had been speaking with a man's voice and swearing obscenities (demonic symptoms pictured in the movie). She'd had the face of Satan as she leered and spat.

This was apparently what the mother saw. What I saw was a terrified child who was bewildered by her mother's screaming. Tears ran down the child's face as she tried to make sense of her mother's hysteria.

As I reached to pick up the little girl, her mother warned me to be careful of her, for the demons were in charge. But the child, terrified out of her wits over her mother's behavior, reached for me. She came to me so readily. I don't believe she would have ordinarily, but she was so frightened of the wild behavior of her mother, she had no other course to follow.

I do believe demonic ends may have been served, but it was not the little girl who was acting in so erratic and evil a manner. So after I had lifted up the girl, I prayed for all demonic behavior—which is not the same as demonic possession—to be driven from her mother. I asked Jesus "in the name of his shed blood" to cleanse the demons of hysteria and fear. He did! Soon the mother relaxed and smiled. Her lower chin was trembling and her hands were a bit shaky, but I handed her daughter back to her, grateful that she at last reached for her daughter. They embraced. The crisis was past. I said yet another prayer, blessing the home with peace. And when everything seemed settled I left.

I have thought many times of that odd night. I do not believe the little girl was possessed. I don't even believe the mother— hysterical as she was—was possessed. I do believe in the power of suggestion from the film *The Exorcist*. It had led the mother into a highly susceptible state of mind. Satan held a reign of terror in a mind that gave itself too readily to the film. And I do believe I was able to help ease a satanic state of fear. No demons were exorcised, but the peace of Christ drove out an unrealistic psychosis. Never again (as far as I know) did that mother ever cause her child to be afraid.

But I also remember a needy young man who committed suicide. He too was a member of our church. I remember thinking how troubled he was and how little I did to effect his healing. He called the church one morning and with pistol in hand, talked to one of the other ministers on our staff. While he talked to the minister he pulled the trigger and killed himself.

Was he demon possessed? No. Was Satan delighted that he had destroyed a beautiful life? Yes, I think so. For the lonely pain felt by this beautiful but tortured boy was demonic. Because of that demonic pain he destroyed himself.

I cannot escape two convictions. First, that to challenge Satan, the author of all mental splintering, is definitely one way we may be able to help people back to mental health. I am not a psychologist but I have always tried to perform mental miracles that would keep the world from psychotic disintegration and pain.

The second truth I face is how often Jesus helped people from mental anguish to health. Even of Legion's demonaic, this great healing miracle is finished with a healed man sitting clothed and in his right mind. Jesus is pre-Freudian—1,800 years pre, but He often called on God to heal all whose healthy minds had fallen under the control of Satan.

And here is the great lesson for the church. What can we do to help psychiatrists and psychologists? We may eagerly enter our splintering world intent on seeing what we may do to call the world to peace. Too often churches have mocked psychiatrists as odd doctors and shrinks. Jokes, often told by Christians, are libeled at these well-meaning, trained healers. The church needs to remember that where there is no peace Satan is in charge. And where Satan is in charge is deceit. We must not be at odds with others who seek to heal. As Jesus boldly touched the hurting minds of His day, may we be ready to order Satan out of the bleeding souls of our day. Miracles in a sense are our business and a miracle occurs each time we touch the broken with understanding and concern.

Conclusion

A word of caution: As I mentioned before, Christians must not be over-eager to label mental illness as demon possession. Most forms of mental illness are unrelated to demons. Many forms are neurochemical in nature. Others have extreme environmental or hereditary roots. But some evangelicals have sought to label every addiction as demon possession. It was not uncommon during the 1980s to hold exorcisms to cast out the demon of alcoholism and five-card stud. Alcoholics and Gamblers Anonymous would probably have been a better, fairer treatment.

But Jesus is the great miracle worker and when we can help we should, by invoking the Savior's peace over troubled minds— whatever the source. Just the sensitivity to want to help may be the miracle we need to heal our troubled world. Not every illness must be met with dramatic exorcism. After all, miracles of every sort spring up from the soil of true compassion. And Jesus is the Healer.

CHAPTER NINE

Miracles: God's Way of Saying We Matter

What's a miracle, Andy?
God.
That's all?
God payin' attention to you.
SANDRA PRATT MARTIN

Author William March's unknown soldier, wounded and wallowing in the barbed wire, was put to death by a kind German officer. As his eyes fluttered closed, the soldier said, "I have broken the chain . . . I have defeated the inherent stupidity of life."

Death is the end of every empty human routine? It is a deliverance in all such cases. If I die with no understanding of why I was born I cannot triumph over existence. If I have no faith, emptiness will mock my purpose for living. If I have no reason to live this life, I will find little hope in the next.

I came to believe long ago that a universe without the God of miracles is a black hole where all idealism is sucked into the dark whirlpool of human arrogance and a pointless lust for purpose.

Erase God and whatever is, is moral. Tyranny is as right as love. Nuclear war is as wholesome as peace. Altruism is indulgence. Sacrifice is hedonism.

If I should abandon faith I would be left to the caprice of such pointlessness that my despair would be certain. I would be but a prisoner of natural law. So I choose to believe in miracles. Miracles let God out of the box of our disbelief. There *is* hope. Miracles stand up to natural law, shouting that it may not master my mood. Each time God leaves His imprisonment in that box we call "the laws of nature," He makes it clear that He prizes us above the mere order of things in his universe. The only alternative to believing that I am special to God is nihilism. Nihilism is a harsh worldview in which I weep before an orderly but pointless universe and cry, "Is anybody out there who cares about my tears?"

Nihilism spawns an insatiable hunger to believe that I count. Across from the wonder of God's love of me lies the horror of emptiness that comes to all who refuse to believe in miracles. When I begin to doubt, I am prone to assume terrible arrogance. Without God in my life I become a god to myself. Without the belief that God exists to do mighty things, I am soon lowered to worshiping my own petty achievements. I grow dull and empty. This should not surprise me. Bleakness always comes from substituting my self-importance for God's glory.

Secular thinkers often embody the arrogance I fear. Humanists usurp the place of God, crying, "Isn't it true that man has come a long way on his evolutionary climb from the amoeba to the stars? Since we cannot celebrate the fatherhood of God, may we not at least praise the creative courage of those godless, triumphant souls who rise on the bright wings of their discoveries—moving ever upward in the lonely universe?"

But secular humanism is not a triumphant philosophy. Depression is rampant in our day. How did we come to think so poorly of ourselves in the West? Though we thrive on sweet abundance, the mood at our table is sour. Those who live without God smile, but it is usually nothing more than a grinning pessimism. Our abundance depresses us. Heavy with possessions, space-age men and women often whimper themselves to sleep in their gilded dwellings of despair.

As the West moved from a religious worldview to a secular one, God became more remote. Between Galileo and Carl Sagan, the universe expanded infinitely. In learning the universe's dimension, we have come to feel a need to micro-size both ourselves and God. As the Inquisitor in Bertolt Brecht's study of Galileo confessed:

My child, it seems that God has blessed our modern astronomers with imaginations. It is quite alarming! Do you know that the earth—which we old fogies supposed to be so large—has shrunk to something no bigger than a walnut, and the new universe has grown so fast and prelates—and even cardinals—look like ants. Why, God Almighty might lose sight of a Pope!

Such scientific conclusions have driven us to the brink of despair, and existential philosophy has pushed us over. Secular evolution teaches that we came from nothing. And popular philosophy denies us any life beyond. Having zeroes for both our origin and destiny, the only conclusion that can be reached is that life is a great void.

But when God passes a miracle, we become a people of meaning. We prop up our sad predicament with hope. Somebody out there cares.[55]

My own war against meaninglessness has been won by a great God who uses miracles to teach me just how special I am to Him. I don't have to slash at senselessness with bourbon, cocaine, a new car, bigger boats, or a more spacious house. I don't have to bare my soul in endless therapy and while away the cold night of my existence with giddy laughter. God is on my side. He has performed extraordinary wonders to show me His love. I can quit asking, "Is anybody home in the universe?" The Holy Spirit whispers to me, "Go ahead! Ring the bell! God will answer the door with a miracle to show you how much you mean to Him."

Miracles: Proof That We Count With God

Save is a big word with both me and God. Jesus called himself the "Saver" or "Savior." God is out to rescue me with hope. So why did I start feeling hopeless in the first place? Because I feel I am enmeshed in circumstances I cannot change. Why can't I change them? Because I am too small; my entanglements are too large— to change them would require a miracle.

But things are not as hopeless as I feel they are. God does care. Miracles say loud and clear that I count with Him. When the apostles were afraid of the storm, Jesus came to them walking on the water. How did he do it? He suspended the laws of gravitation and buoyancy. This miracle proved how valuable his friends were to him. The same thing was true when the Israelites were trapped on the shores of the Red Sea. Because Israel meant so much to God, He simply suspended the laws of nature and the Red Sea behaved unnaturally or, rather, supernaturally. That's what miracles do: They set aside the laws of nature so God can serve the best interest of his friends. In this same way He proves how much I mean to Him.

Consider Jesus' first miracle. Why did He change the water into wine? Simply because His friends were in trouble with their social image at a wedding where they had not been thorough in their planning. John 2:11 says that this was the "beginning of miracles did Jesus in Cana of Galilee, and manifested forth His glory; and His disciples believed on Him" (KJV). This miracle seemed to depend upon the faith of the servants as much as on the faith of Mary. Jesus told the servants to fill the pots with water. They did. Then He told them to draw some water out and take it to the master of the banquet. They did. Somewhere between the well and the master's taste buds, the water became wine. Everyone agreed that Jesus' wine was the best at the wedding.

Of course, we would expect Jesus' wine to be the best. What seems noteworthy about this miracle is that it was a group venture of faith. Mary, Jesus' mother, believed Jesus could do it. The servants obediently collected the water, believing that Jesus could do it. The master of the banquet tasted the wine, smiled, and then said something in Aramaic that can only be translated as "Wow!" in English. So this miracle actually became a group project of faith. And from that faith came the realization that God cares.

I have discovered that when I add my thimble-full of faith to that of others, our collective faith becomes a mighty force. Group miracles are always the most meaningful. It's nice when a faith healer, all by himself, does something so wonderful and authentic that no one can doubt it. When any group of Christians becomes part of the miraculous answer, things are even better. When many people become part of the answer to an impossible problem, the miraculous can descend on an entire congregation with great force.

And so I am in love with a God who outdoes His own natural law to show me how much I mean to Him. I can see that nature is often kind. When it is, I see God in the seagull's nest or the mountain stream. But what about when nature is not kind? What conclusions am I to draw when quakes rip cities or villages are decimated with the plague? Do I say God is a fiend who cares nothing for me? Of course not!

Nature alone is not the best way God can say, "I love you." It is by suspending the less kind parts of nature that God demonstrates how much I really mean to Him. For example, Jesus ended Bartimaeus's blindness and gave him sight by a supernatural act. The miracle proved that Bartimaeus was important to God. Jesus fed the five thousand because He had compassion on the hungry crowd. In considering such supernatural events we see our cosmic importance, without a God who gets involved in the natural world we are but unimportant microbes. Author Andre Malraux said, "The greatest mystery is not that we have been flung at random among the profusion of the earth and the galaxy of the stars, but that in this prison we can fashion images of ourselves sufficiently powerful to deny our nothingness." But I know he is only partly right. I would be nothing if I were not loved by God.[56]

When I was a child, the monsters of the dark seemed real and fanged, lurking in the hallway just outside my door. I heard thunderous footfalls in the gloom. But I slept well after I discovered those footfalls were only my mother who heard me crying and came to comfort me. I never saw her in the darkness, but I felt her touch and knew she was there.

Miracles are my touch from God in the darkness. The universe may appear vast and cold, but I am not alone. I know this because there are many unexplainable wonders that make this possible. Did they all happen way back there in Bible times? Of course not. What kind of God would God be if He loved only the people of distant generations and ignored the people at hand? I realize that beginning with Luther and Calvin there has been a large group of scholars who say all miracles ended with the close of the New Testament area. But it is an odd notion that sees God acting only in the distant past to prove that only ancient hurting people had special meaning to Him. Not so. God continues actively redeeming the hurting present moment. Consider the following account:

> As a baby only seven months old, Emily Weichman had a stroke. While it was the only stroke she ever had, she remained a weak child never enjoying a robust state of health. In September 1991, the Weichmans were driving across Wyoming. They were in a mostly deserted area when Emily said, "Mommy, I'm sick!" Soon thereafter, she began to vomit. The Weichmans suddenly knew the grip of fear. They knew Emily must be taken to a hospital at once. But how? They were in a desolate and unpopulated area. Then a wonderful thing happened. Suddenly everyone began to see those wonderful blue and white markers. They passed at least four of these signs which led them right to a hospital. Emily's condition was quickly diagnosed. Her life was spared. The hospital attendants stabilized her with anticonvulsant drugs.
>
> Once Emily was in her room, Mrs. Weichman told the doctor, "If it weren't for those hospital signs we might still be driving around."
>
> The physician was dumbfounded. "What signs?"
>
> "The ones lining our route," Marlene explained. "They were literally a lifesaver—we couldn't have found the hospital without them."

The doctor was perplexed. "I live about eight miles out on that road. I travel it every day here," he told her. "I've never seen any hospital signs."

Marlene was puzzled. No hospital signs! But all four adults in the van had seen them.

The next day Marlene phoned the Rock Springs Chamber of Commerce to ask about the elusive signs. "There have never been any hospital signs along that route," said a city official.

Emily is now healthy and happy. Her parents consider her a "miracle child."[57]

Now, Luther and Calvin would have said this didn't happen since there have been no miracles since the New Testament era. But why would God, who performed miracles for the apostles— as in Jesus calming the storm—not care equally for the Weichmans? Such preferential love in most ways stands against all I believe about God.

There are miracles! I am loved! In the present age God still does wonderful things for me. Miracles were not written down in Scripture just to hear the audience "ooh and ahh!" They were written to show us God cares.

Reason to Live, Reason to Die

Victor Frankl escaped the horrors of the Auschwitz death camp determined to deal with the why of existence. During his imprisonment he saw life stripped to the stark minimum. With little reason to hope, he forged a philosophy of hope. He observed that those under rigorous deprivations abandoned all interest in sex (a primal drive, contrary to Freud). The tortured did not pursue any hope of power (the preoccupation of Alfred Adler). One thing alone survived in the death camp: hope. Meaning remained quite alive within the gaunt inmates of Auschwitz, for they never quit hoping, no matter how little reason they had for it. And Auschwitz, for all its evil, was not just a house of horrors; it was also a place where miracles did happen. The grief and horror was punctuated, even if infrequently, by tales of God's grace.

Victor Frankl has alluded to a survey taken in France in which 89 percent of the people polled admitted that everybody needs something to live for. Also, 61 percent of those interviewed said that there was somebody or some issue for which they were willing to die. Jean-Baptiste Clamence in Albert Camus's *The Fall* might not have rated God very high as something for which one would die. But the apostle Paul would roundly disagree: "For to me to live is Christ, and to die is gain" (Phillippians 1:21). Paul himself would count the times that proved his specialness to God. For example, in Acts 28:4–6 Paul's bite from a snake— perhaps a cobra—did not kill him. That miracle certainly attested to God's love.

While Frankl, being Jewish, did not say that "ultimate meaning" is Christ, he did say it is spiritual. His therapy is not psychotherapy (mind therapy) but logotherapy—that is *meaning* therapy. Logotherapy, said Frankl, dares to enter the spiritual side of human existence. Interpreting this statement in a Christian context is our only hope of confronting our meaninglessness with miracles. God has done wondrous things to prove how much we mean to Him. It was for this reason that Jesus came out of the grave: to prove our hopelessness would dissolve in this triumphant miracle.

How desperate I am to believe I count—to find a real reason to live! Even the most rigid determinists from time to time would

mysteries of God. Would I then not lord it over all the rest of those who had not managed my understanding? Would I not be prone to boast, "Come see my little God and my graphs that chart his thoughts"?

To fight against either miracles or mystery is foolish. The miracles of my faith contain within them a reply all its own for my skepticism. As a miracle-believing Christian I cannot prove the existence of God by using my Bible. But neither can an atheist answer their own set of mysteries. Which question is easier to answer, the mystery of the Trinity or the origin of the universe without God?

The atheist Robert Ingersoll once met the great Congregational pastor Henry Ward Beecher. Ingersoll was renowned for his militant unbelief and his cutting debates with the pious, where he nearly always managed to "prove" there was no God. They once met in Beecher's study in Plymouth Church in Boston. A part of the decor of the study was a beautifully made celestial globe—an attractive piece of art, meticulously constructed. Ingersoll scrutinized it and said, "Henry, that's magnificent! Who made it?" The pastor answered with sparkling wit, "Why, Robert, nobody made it; it just happened."

Ingersoll and Beecher represent two poles, faith and antifaith. Some, like Ingersoll, have a know-it-all attitude toward the miracle of creation. But they cannot answer all questions satisfactorily. There are great mysteries about creation, destiny, and meaning they cannot reconcile. Neither can they answer many questions about personality, psyche, or guilt. For all such doubters the universe itself is there, but without meaning.

Perhaps the major difference between Christians and skeptics is this: Christians accept a mysterious God and the universe is solved. Atheists deny God and must therefore live in a mysterious universe.

But the greatest barrier to skeptics' salvation is the failure of Christians to confront doubt with bold faith. We have kept the Christ in the crypt. The world is suspicious of all mention of God out of the proper gothic context. Thus Jesus, like a medieval Bible, still in some ways seems chained to the church.

Peter, on his way into the city one day, passed a crippled man in a cranny of the city wall. In compassion and, more importantly, in the sunlight and fresh air of the outside world, he said to the man, "In the name of Jesus!" (Acts 3:6). Today the cripple would probably say, "Please, not here. Everyone is staring. Let's do it some other way—I'll meet you on Easter after church."

What happened that day was a thing of beauty. The lame man walked, even leaped. It all happened because the name of Jesus was spoken in courage to a hopeless soul who in the end, flinging his paraphernalia in the ecstasy of his wholeness, was able to run. He ran because it seemed the thing to do when he had never done it before. He ran because Peter had caused him to "ingest" a new inner Christ who set him free to be whole. He heard this inner Christ cry, "Run, man! Let them know there is power in Jesus' name. Run if you love God. Let them doubt that your mind has strength, but not your ankles. Run! *Run! RUN!*"

How desperately the church needs to learn that there is miraculous power in the name of Jesus when spoken in the sunlit world outside the church. That name can still set the dumb to singing and cripples sprinting through a host of cynics. Jesus Himself lived freely in the era of the Caesars, striding His world with power and dignity, healing and meaning. So why, in these latter times, should I subdue Him and force Him to live in the dark, presiding over my solemn and candlelit assemblies? Like a captured animal, the liturgical Christ roars against our euphonies, ready to escape the church house and meet the needs of the suffering and the damned who lie beyond. He protests our artificial categories of *sacred* and *secular*. The miracle-working Christ is a reason to live—for an individual or a world.

Conclusion

One day Helen Keller's teacher placed in her hand the key that was to unlock her silent blackness. Neither hearing nor seeing since early childhood, Helen had no way to learn or communicate. She had touched hundreds of objects, but there was no way to know what they were without sight and sound.

One day, her teacher took her down a familiar path to the well house where someone was drawing water. Her teacher let the cold water run over one hand and in sign language spelled into her other hand the word W-A-T-E-R. Suddenly Helen felt a symbol of something stirring in the gray darkness of her consciousness. Suddenly she came alive. She had only a single word composed of five letters. But that single word set her free at last from the dumb prison of herself. Suddenly she knew that, like water, everything in the world had a name. She left the well house alive with the new possibility of becoming a real, communicating person in a world that opened to her all at once.

Young Helen might have appeared strange to any who saw her in ecstasy, but she was thrilled with what she called "a detonation." A silent, dumb absurd world was exploding with singing life and she was in the middle of it all.[58]

Christ has been the detonation for many lives. In fact, my own testimony of Him would be one like Helen Keller's: Christ for me brought a new light and joy, and all the world I knew at last made sense because of Him. Life for me is new every morning because Christ ever makes all things new.

In times of doubt I need only to remember that with Christ life becomes bearable. More than bearable—hopeful. Christ and emptiness, like fire and water, cannot occupy the same space at one time. He stands ever at the door of my doubting soul and knocks. And I quickly lift the latch and welcome Him. When He enters He shatters my bondage to ordinary living. He smashes my hopelessness with God's hammer of mystery.

There are still millions whose lives are devoid of meaning. They are starved people who live in a plain world going nowhere. They worship only a captive God too little to do anything miraculous. It is time for a detonation.

CHAPTER TEN

The Final Wonder: The World on Fire

Silence settles on the clocks,
Nursing mothers point a sly
Index finger at a sky
Crimson with the setting sun;
In the valley of the fox
Gleams the barrel of a gun.

W. H. AUDEN

The greatest of all God's miracles is yet to come. God is about to raise the curtain on history's final act—the great wrap-up of Time. All of God's miracles have their moment in history and history has always been headed in one direction. The world's new beginning was first announced at Jesus' resurrection. And the final wonders of God's Apocalypse yet to come promises to be as exciting as his creation. It amazes me how this impending finish has long occupied the creative philosophers and poets, some in delighted expectation, some with hopelessness. W. B. Yeats once wrote:

Turning and turning in the widening gyre
The falcon cannot hear the falconer;

Things fall apart; the center cannot hold;
Mere anarchy is loosed upon the world,
The blood-dimmed tide is loosed, and everywhere
The ceremony of innocence is drowned.[59]

With an even more perceptive eye Tennyson a half-century earlier wrote:

For I dipp'd into the future, far as human eye could see,
Saw the Vision of the world, and all the wonder that would be:
Saw the heavens fill with commerce, argosies of magic sails,
Pilots of the purple twilight, dropping down with costly bales;
Heard the heavens fill with shouting, and there rained a ghastly
    dew
From the nations' airy navies grappling in the central blue.[60]

Judith Deem Dupree wrote:

We shall hear a Voice of splendor echo through our halls,
Shake the portals of our being—
Separate the walls.[61]

An unknown prophet wrote:

When pictures look alive with movement free.
When men like fishes swim beneath the sea.
When men outstripping birds scan the sky,
Then half-the-world sore drenched in blood shall lie.

And George Vandeman wrote:

Down the minster aisles of splendor, from betwixt the cherubim,
Through the wondering throng with motion strong and fleet

Sounds his victor tread approaching with a music far and dim,
The music of the coming of his feet.

Sandaled not with sheen of silver, girded not with woven gold,
Weighted not with shimmering gems and odors sweet,
But white winged and shod with glory in the tabor light of old,
The glory of the coming of his feet.

He is coming, O my friend, with his everlasting peace,
With his blessedness, immortal and complete,
He is coming, O my friend, and his coming brings release,
I listen for the coming of his feet.[62]

Slouching Toward Sodom

Several years ago Robert Bourke suggested that we were *Slouch-ing Toward Gomorrah.* For reasons of political correctness Bourke could not call his book—even in metaphor—*Slouching Toward Sodom* where the Sodomites lived. Sodom and Gomorrah were twin cities, however. So, I'd like to ask how *Gomorrahites* (or the *Gomorraheans*) would have felt about Bourke's title? My suspicions are that they would resent the title, preferring the title *Slouching Toward Chicago.*

But Gomorrah is probably only us. I used to think that there was a big sign outside Gomorrah that read, "The Wickedest City in the World! Depraved is US!" But having viewed the human race's uncanny ability at self-congratulation, I now believe that Gomorrah—as it saw itself—was a very normal, somewhat moral city.

I have known only a few truly wicked people but even their wickedness faded a bit as I got to know them. And even the most wicked people I have read about almost always saw themselves as free, live-and-let-live people. So in Gomorrah I can only imagine they saw themselves as the Pride of the Valley. The Gomorrah stock exchange was bullish on Sodom. Their plays were rated to keep theater safe for the children. Their homeless were a constant urban focus. Spear-control was a constant concern, and all minorities—and every sexual preference, as Sodom could attest—was honored. There was no glass ceiling in commerce or industry. All pride organizations were proud.

What, they must have thought, is the possibility of Apocalypse in a culture where everything is coming up roses?

And so too does our own world think. "How could God strike us?" we murmur as we leave our churches on Sunday. But in our hearts we know this final wonder of wonders will come upon the world, like a thief in the night. Our intrigue about this, our earth's finality, has filled the novel shelves of America's bookstores. The current rash of second-coming novels has now sold in the neighborhood of forty million copies. According to some recent studies, fifty percent of Americans believe all the prophecies of the Book of Revelation will come true. Thirty-six percent of Americans believe that the end of the world will come in the manner the *Left Behind* series suggests.

In anticipation of this final wonder God has called the Church to work—the hard rescue work of loving Gomorrah. Why would God call His Church to this mission? Because He loves Gomorrah. It might be argued that brimstone seems to be a funny way for God to show His love. But remember long ago the angels once haggled with Abraham outside of Sodom, trying to find a way to save it.

Alas, sometimes cultures must be "allowed" to die. It happens when cultures make no difference in the world they are called to serve. In a sense these cultures destroy themselves as they gradually become indulgent, immoral, self-seeking, and uncaring of every important dream of God. Belshazzar didn't see the handwriting on the wall until Babylon had come to the place where it was making no significant impact for anything important. And God let the Medes conquer Babylon so they could have a go at doing things better.

Our job is to take up the mantle of helping to save, or at least reform, our own Babylons, our own Gomorrahs.

Dr. Laessic, an old German professor at OBU, a school I once attended, told a fascinating story of his attempt to missionize in Africa in the 1930s. He had gone into a particular tribal village to minister to them. It was his custom to build a bamboo school and then within its open interior to reduce the various sounds of the tribal language to an alphabet and then set about translating the words into readable English letters. Once the language had been redacted to letters, he would begin to evangelize in an attempt to tell others about Christ.

In every village where he began the process, there was always his first and primary enemy—the witch doctor. It was this tribal mystic that always came and forbade him the beginning of his educational ministry, trying to drive the missionary out of town. In one particular tribal village, Dr. Laessic was confronted by a witch doctor who challenged him to take his belongings and get out of the village. When Dr. Laessic refused, the witch doctor said, "If you do not leave this village, tonight an evil god will strike your little school with lightning and burn it to the ground."

The eyes of the villagers grew round with the excitement of such a fiery display and such a battle between the good God of the Christian missionary and the evil gods of the witch doctor. Dr. Laessic confessed to us all that he was not so much afraid of the dark god as he was the witch doctor. He propped himself up against a tree to watch for the witch doctor to come upon his little school in the middle of the night and put it to the torch.

At about three o'clock in the morning, he said, while he remained on the alert for the witch doctor, there was a terrifying crack of thunder and a single bolt of lightning fell with blinding, ear-splitting intensity upon the school. Fire shot out through he thatched roof, and before long the entire school was ablaze. The intensity of the light and the heat summoned the villagers from their huts and all came out and watched as the witch doctor gloated over his victory and Dr. Laessic despaired.

Early the next morning the villagers, led by the witch doctor, came to Dr. Laessic and demanded that he leave their village. Dr. Laessic then said, "I will leave the village tomorrow if you still want me to leave. But today I will spend myself in prayer to the true and living God, and tonight he will strike the evil shrine in the center of the village with lightning and burn it to the ground."

After he had made the statement, Dr. Laessic immediately thought in his heart, "What have I said?" He couldn't believe he had promised that God would burn down the pagan shrine in the center of the village. He confessed that he then entered into the most ardent prayer of his entire life. He didn't ask God for a particularly big bolt of lightning. In fact, he told God that it could be a measly little spark. He really didn't care much about the size of the lightning. "But God," he confessed, "while I wished I hadn't put you on the spot like this, both of us are going to look pretty bad if you don't back me up."

He prayed on. Then, at about 3:00 in the morning, as he continued to pray and feel increasingly bad that he had put God on the spot, a second flash of light came, with an even more horrendous clap of thunder, and shook the village. The evil shrine was aflame with the glory of a great God—whom I suspect would like us to put him on such a spot far more often than we do.

The next morning when the villagers came to the door, Dr. Laessic was able to issue the old challenge from 1 Kings 18:21 and 24: "How long will you falter between two opinions; if the Lord be God then follow him, but if Baal be God then follow him! . . . The God who answers by fire, He is God!"

Apocalypse and Our Final Hope

Come, let us stand back and see the never-ending salvation of the Lord. When will God begin these celestial fireworks of His? When there is no other way out of the morass. Miracles always come when somebody somewhere is in a cul-de-sac of extreme need. God has been rescuing His people for many years. As He rescued Israel from the Pharoah's soldiers and Paul from the jail cell, He will no doubt send His Apocalypse when we find ourselves in some sort of celestial pinch. We are marching slowly toward that final need for help. Historian Arnold Toynbee stands as a grim reminder that twenty-eight world civilizations have already perished and that the American civilization seems queued up in the same line waiting its turn at irrelevance. Neal Postman, in his book *Amusing Ourselves to Death,* said there are four cities that represent the history of America. The first was Boston, which represents revolutionary America. The second is New York, which represents immigrant America. The third is Chicago, which represents industrial America. And the fourth is Las Vegas, which stands for the entertainment culture. We can only wonder if "couch potatoism" and the dawn of apocalypse are not bedfellows.

But the Christian view of history has taught me not to live in fear of the end. I am not to be morosely over-occupied with it or forget that it is a sure and forthcoming event. Of course, like most Christians in my own smug view of discipleship, I once believed that before things got really rough at time's fiery finale, I would be whisked out of the arena of suffering. I wouldn't have to worry anyway! It wasn't until later that it occurred to me that Christian martyrs die daily in other parts of the world. These could not afford the luxury of my hoped for escape. Instead, they saw their tribulation as the opportunity for proving Christ's steadfastness in crisis. Remember, tribulation has been the mode of discipleship since Paul and Peter died under the persecution of Nero 1950 years ago. As Jesus died in pain to the glory of God, there is no real reason for me as a Christian to believe I can avoid such suffering. What right do I have to believe that the trumpet will sound and the great "whoosh" will come and I and all other "lucky" followers will be suctioned from the desperate planet just before firefall?

I cannot allow the current and popular form of doomsdayism to divert me from the true faith, from which my hope stems: Jesus is coming again.

Of course, many people throughout the ages have held out hope, and not always in line with popular expectations. During all the recent apocalyptic fury over Y2K, I was reminded of Radulph Gläber, who in the year 999 believed the world was coming to an end. He was committed to the coming of Christ at the stroke of midnight, January 1, 1000 A.D. He fancifully described the Mass by which the pope on that New Year's Eve would break the bread, believing that as the unleavened bread snapped in his fingers, Jesus would settle over the Lateran in Rome (the Vatican had not been built yet, for this reason and others some scholars doubt Gläber's story. Also the calendar had not been redated as yet). But Y1K ended pretty much like Y2K: Jesus didn't show.

On February 21, 1431, Jean d'Arc went on trial. She came under the court's scrutiny for her dreams of apocalypse and her partnership with Christ in the subjugation of the England to the cross. She was burned as a witch before she could publish her view of history.

The fifth monarchists in 1656 believed that the recently deposed Charles I would be replaced by the Second Coming of Christ who would take the throne of England in 1660. Jesus didn't take the throne, Charles II did.

In the nineteenth century the Millerites picked a mountain and, dressed in white, ascended and waited. Alas, they came back down the mountain to form in time a brand of Adventism that would change the world in wonderful ways even if their mountain-climbing rapture rehearsal did not bag the Savior.

As a child I can remember how every tent evangelist believed Hitler was the antichrist. He came as close as any character in a current novel to matching Christ's adversary. In my childhood I was taken in by this idea. I believed Hitler would be the antichrist. But he died, as did all the prophets who predicted him to be the henchman of history.

By the time I was in seminary, Hal Lindsay had teamed up with C. C. Carlson to write the *Late, Great Planet Earth*. I read Lindsay, convinced that I would never live to collect my Social Security. With the world as it was, I figured, how could it continue much longer? The European Common Market was already fornicating with the great Harlot—as Lindsay saw the world—even as I read Lindsay's book!

Now, of course, I'm a little embarrassed that I gave so much credibility to Lindsay, who became a millionaire while I bought his mistaken views. Three months ago I went on Social Security and I cannot locate my old worrisome volume of Lindsay's.

Across recent decades lay the prophecies of those who sought to prove the antichrists of their day. Marx, Kaiser Bill, Stalin, Hitler, Ho Chi Minh, Henry Kissinger, the Maharishi . . . Some evangelicals even suggested that the gay-friendly theme parks of Orlando were the sure sign Disney's culture of Tomorrowland was the culture of Gomorrah. I even read one treatise that said if you assigned Greek numerals to the English letters of Mickey Mouse, you would come up with 666. Poor little mouse! The whole thing boggles the mind.

But, as I said, none of these mistaken views must be allowed to usurp the doctrine of final wonder. Jesus is coming again. It has always been the theme of the church. And we must not let all who "under-define" its glory diminish its inevitability. The hope of the church is the certainty of God's final promise. We would all do better to get up each morning and breathe the final words of Revelation, "Even so, come quickly, Lord Jesus!" But until Jesus does come, we must be prepared to enter our world, changing it with generous doses of ministry and holiness. It is less important to understand when Jesus is coming and more important to minister in his name till he actually does show up.

"It's Closing Time!"

A friend of mine recently sent me a cartoon that I've not been able to get out of my mind. The cartoon pictures a bearded, scrawny prophet, clad like John the Baptist. He is a doomsday prophet, holding a sign that says, "The end is not near. You must learn to cope."

This is to say that although we should always cling to our hope in Jesus, we should not become apocalypse junkies. I was going into a shopping center in North Carolina a couple of years ago in August. The sun blistered the asphalt. To step from my air-conditioned auto onto the parking lot was like the first step across the threshold of hell. It was then that I saw a young man standing on the sidewalk. He carried a sign that read, "Christians will go through the tribulation." His shirt was soaked with his sweat. He was paying a miserable price for his witness.

I barely restrained myself from going up to him and saying, "Son, even if you are right about the tribulation, why start early?" He was paying a heavy price just to straighten out all the apocalyptic novel readers. I wanted to take him out of the sun and buy him a Coke. I wanted to tell him that it is as bad to fall over backward as to fall on your face. I wanted to tell him to eat a little popcorn, watch a little television—take a load off. Come back to the planet and lets be friends while we wait for Jesus.

I can't help wondering why God would have made such a beautiful world if He didn't want us to live in it and enjoy it while we waited for the fire to fall. And I have asked myself, "If I were God, what kind of world would I want my Son to come back to? One where everyone about to be raptured was heavy with WWJD jewelry and Second Coming bumper stickers? Or one where Christians were working with non-Christians to lead them Godward, with a reasonable lifestyle grounded in adoration and a commitment to God that did not embarrass Him.

So far I've never climbed a mountain dressed in white to wait it out for Jesus. But I think I have passed a lot of people who just got back from the climb. I think there's a sadder but wiser look about them. What is nice is that they, like myself, have a moderated view of the final fireworks.

I want the casual attitude of the NBC anchorman whose newscast in the '70s included a coverage of the Hindu forecast of the end of the world on February 11. "If the world does end on February 11," he said, "NBC will bring you full coverage on the twelfth." NBC had a final view that seems to agree with Martin Luther, who said, "Even if I knew Jesus was coming tomorrow, I would plant an apple tree today." So I am by choice a gardener. I love what sunlight and rain does to my plants. And I am content to simply tend to my field.

The Ring of Fire

When I was a child, a bunch of us gathered around the old Loomis house on a very windy day. Mr. Loomis was a huge man with a fearsome demeanor and we children in the neighborhood were very afraid of him. He seemed the kind of man who would spring upon us in the darkness, like Freddie on Elm Street. He made brooms and had huge knives that cut the hard straw but might just as easily cut up little Baptist and Pentecostal children. So we usually kept far away from his house.

But for reasons of our own we children gathered in his yard and began playing an interesting game with matches. We would each take a match and light it and throw it in the dry grass. Then we would let the circle of fire grow until it reached a very large size and then we would all work at stamping it out. The winners were those who never called in for help and who confidently stamped out the flame which began to be driven by the wind.

This day, I determined I would be the grand winner and so I lit the grass on fire and let the circle of fire grow until it was apocalyptically large. Then I began to try to stamp it out. But alas the wind had stiffened to a gale and the fire had spread too far. I was no longer able to stamp it out. I panicked with horror as I watched the growing circle of fire move up to Mr. Loomis's house and travel up the corner onto the walls. While the raging flames ate at his house, Mr. Loomis came out. I shrunk back in terror from the huge white-bearded man who glared at me.

My mother ended up calling the fire department. My little friend Frances told me that while I had won the contest on setting the largest fire, I was sure to be put in prison for life, and they'd never let my mother in to see me. I asked my mother if I would have to go to prison, and when she said she hoped so, I broke into tears.

But of this I cannot doubt. I learned that day the overwhelming secret of fire. Fire is deliriously intoxicating in its hunger to devour. Somewhere between premillennial theology and T. S. Eliot's *Wasteland* must lie the encroaching ring of fire. We may be on the edge of apocalypse, and perhaps we should be alert to the footfalls of God as he approaches our time. We must be aware and strain to see him as he comes, in case he is carrying a torch.

Conclusion

Regarding this great wonder with which time will end, I must say "Bully for God!" I'm glad he has made it possible for me to participate in the joy of this promise, whether or not I am still alive at His coming. I take great comfort from being in the company of the apostle Paul. In his younger years he seemed convinced that Jesus was coming during his lifetime. When he wrote the first Christians he was convinced Jesus was coming soon and he would not die. "We shall not all sleep," (1 Corinthians 15:51–52) he wrote, "but we will be changed—in a flash, in the twinkling of an eye, at the last trumpet."

It was perhaps two years later (50 C.E.) that Paul wrote 1 Thessalonians. His view at that time was that he would still be alive when Jesus came again, for he wrote, "We who are alive, who are left till the coming of the Lord, will not precede those who have fallen asleep. For the Lord himself will come down from heaven with a loud command, with the voice of the arch-angel and with the trumpet call of God, and the dead in Christ will rise first. After that, we who are still alive will be caught up together with them in the clouds to meet the Lord in the air (see 1 Thessalonians 4:15–17).

But an older Paul put this final wonder at a distance in 2 Timothy 4:6–8, when he expected to be offered on the high altar of martyrdom. It is clear he still longs for "the appearing of Christ" (see 2 Timothy 4:8), but that he fully expected to die before that event came to pass.

Who does not identify with the apostle's pilgrimage? In his fiery younger days Paul would have been more likely to read Second Coming novels, had they been popular. But in his latter years, he was a steadier, more realistic, apostle. He had no doubt watched a lot of good second-coming believers die scanning the skies with their hope unrealized (2 Thessalonians 4:15). Now he knew he would likely join them. This latter, more temperate, view leads me to wonder if on the day of his death he might not have been out planting apple trees.

As we ready ourselves for the event, let us do so with a patient waiting (see Psalm 40:1). Patient waiting may not sell novels or bumper stickers, but it does sell immense packages of goodwill to those who wait for the Coming without stocking up on bracelets and signs. All in all a positive approach is best. Jesus is coming, and we who pursue a patient waiting are willing to make it easy on God by granting Him his own timetable on the manner.

Some years ago when I was visiting the London dungeon, I saw a fascinating tableau I could not get out of my mind. It was a wax family of plague victims during the epidemic of 1665. There were children affected with plague. The symptoms of the contagion were swellings (*buboes:* hence bubonic) in the groin that made them feel as though they had posies in their pockets. Their fevered faces were red with the temperature. The children (like their parents) knew that there was no cure for Bubonic Plague. When they got it they died! There were no medicines, balms, or therapies that could deliver them. The bishops told them the only chance they had of beating the plague was to be positive in their sickness. If they worried they had no chance, but if they could laugh and dance, maybe they could beat it.

And so the children danced and sang. "Ring A Ring of Roses, (consider their flushed and fevered faces), a pocket full of posies (consider the swelling in their groin), ashes to ashes we all fall down."

I am not intrigued by their song. But I am intrigued that in viewing their end they managed to be positive.

I am ever trying to marry historian Arnold Toynbee to the Apocalypse of John. The twenty-eight civilizations that have preceded my own look rather like a trend to me. I do not believe American culture will be the last to dominate our globe. But Jesus is coming again and God will remain in charge of world history till He does. And to any who would distract me from or hurry me toward this miracle, I must honestly excuse myself. After all, I have an apple tree to plant.

Miracles: Whether We Understand Them or Not The Least We Can Do Is Try to Celebrate Them

Because you have seen me, you have believed: blessed are those who have not seen and yet have believed.

JOHN 20:29

I have tried to write this book in such a way as to combine the truth of biblical miracles and wonders with the probability of miracles in the here and now. My suspicion is that if you didn't believe in contemporary miracles when you began this book, you still don't. If you did, you probably still do. But my fondest hope is that you are content to live in a world where God is all about you. I pray that you will see this God as a real person who grieves over human bondage and takes pleasure in human laughter. If God lives free around you and is able to help you in times of your need, you will no doubt find Him doing wonderful and unbelievable things. When He does, celebrate His love with such an abundance of joy that your peers may see God did not create the world and leave it to fend for itself. God is involved—and where He walks, miracles are His footprints.

In 1977 Judy, a friend of mine, at Sunday worship noticed that an elderly lady in the pew ahead of her had slumped forward and was not moving. My friend ran around the pew and quickly determined the woman was not breathing. She quickly fitted her mouth to that of the silent woman and gave her CPR. After each cycle of breath, she shouted to her, "Breathe, Kate! Breathe, Kate!" After about five minutes the old woman coughed weakly, spit back at her, and opened her eyes. The church by this time had gathered about her, and they broke into applause. It was a heady moment. But was it a miracle? They all say that Kate—who lived another ten years—thought so. And my friend Judy, perhaps thinking of that moment, later wrote these words (in another context):

I sing of life
That seeps into our fissure cells
Beyond our willing.
Cleansing us, claiming us,
Drawing us to deeper yearnings
Than we know.[63]

How Miracles Supply Us with Deeper Yearnings Than We Know

One of my finest pastor friends once lived the kind of hellish life St. Augustine confessed and abandoned. Then, in a kind of theophany, he said, Jesus came to him to demand more of him. He tells the tale in this manner: He was on a "smoke break" in the latrine at North American Aviation when a chum started trying to convince him he needed to "trust Jesus as his Lord." He grew angry and lifted his eyes to tell his friend to leave him alone. But when he did lift his eyes, above the blue collar of his friend's company coveralls shone the face of Christ. Jim lowered his eyes and said, "I believe." It was a long time before he found the courage to lift his eyes for a second look, but when he did his old friend's less regal head was back on his body.

The story of his conversion is rather like that of the Apostle Paul. I believe both stories, primarily because both stories end in men who gave their all—all the rest of their lives—in the full-time service of Christ. Paul told Agrippa: "I was not disobedient to the heavenly vision" (Acts 26:19). I should say he wasn't; from the primary miracle issued a miraculous life and thirteen of the New Testament's twenty-seven books. Neither was my friend Jim disobedient to his heavenly vision. From his vision also issued a lifetime of dedicated Christian ministry. We may test our visions only by the way they order our passions. In the miracle that claimed their lives, both Jim and Paul gave Christ all.

They say old Lazarus never missed a sunrise
After Jesus called him from the cave.
He never missed a single day, they say,
To pass his tomb and laugh across his grave.
He knew the truth: he'd tasted quite a miracle,
For Christ takes cubes and leaves them spherical.

Do I claim too much in this poem of mine? The matter lies in your deciding. But I would encourage you to stay awake. God lingers all around you in the air. Thomas missed the resurrection because he wasn't present when the living Jesus first appeared. So he lived for one week doubting the whole matter. But he was there the next time Christ showed up. Then he believed. It all goes to prove, miracles happen whether or not we're present at the time. The most we might do is try to be there. The least we can do is believe.

Study Questions

INTRODUCTION

God Announcing His Reality in a Predictable World

1. What are the two elements of the "double gift" of miracles?
2. Who was Sysiphus? How does this Greek antihero relate to "the tedium of trivia"? What does this tedium have to do with our lack of self-esteem and spiritual significance?
3. Why do miracles fill us with fear?
4. What is meant by the statement, "Who would want a Savior who couldn't walk on water?"

CHAPTER ONE

Miracles: The Mysterious Force of Faith

1. Why is it said that prayer counts most when we get others to pray for us rather than when we pray for ourselves?
2. Which of our three responses to miracles is the most vital in getting power for living into our inner lives?
3. In this chapter are cited a number of historical miracles. How do such historical miracles lift a nation's spiritual confidence?
4. What does it mean to say that a miracle sets God free from His own laws of nature?

5. What miracle became the focal point of *Ben Hur?* What inspired Lew Wallace to write the movie?

CHAPTER TWO

Miracles: Why Jesus Did Them

1. Why are Jesus' miracles and Jesus' claim to be the Son of God so codependent?
2. What is meant by "pain is a prison"?
3. Why do *touch* and *prayer* in combination release such miracle-working power?
4. Which is really the healer, the evangelist or the sufferer? Why?
5. Explain the relationship between compassion and healing.

CHAPTER THREE

The Virgin Birth Miracle:
How God Came to Planet Earth

1. Why are the Virgin Birth and the Resurrection called the "bookends" of the earthly Christ?
2. What does the term *adoptionism* mean? In what way is it a mere intellectual accommodation to the Virgin Birth?
3. What does the word *theotokos* mean?
4. How do you personally interpret Revelation 12:1–5? Who, in your opinion, is the woman who dominates these verses?
5. Can you differentiate these terms: *Immaculate Conception, Assumption, Perpetual Virginity, Transfiguration?*
6. What do some Christians mean by the "enthronement" of Mary?

CHAPTER FOUR

The Resurrection: The Queen of Miracles

1. What does the name *Anastasia* really mean?
2. Why should we hyphenate *Resurrection-Ascension*? How do the Ascension and the Second Coming relate?
3. How does Paul say the Resurrection creates the Christian faith? Why does he say it?
4. What does George Bernard Shaw call the "Ultimate Statistic"? Why?
5. Why does the New Testament usually refer to the Resurrection in the passive tense?
6. Why was Sunday chosen as the day of Christian worship?
7. Why is the *Resurrection* called the "Queen of Miracles"?

CHAPTER FIVE

Miracles: God Talking Back to a Scientific Age

1. According to a Jewish proverb, why should no one stand at the foot of a sick person's bed?
2. Why have miracles become less impressive in a world crammed with technology?
3. What does it mean to say *technology* is the new, "amoral" god?
4. Why do you think that miracles seem more credible in an animistic world?
5. What led the sixteenth-century Reformers to discount miracles?
6. Why do miracles sponsor the "freedom of God"?
7. Why do you think modern churchgoers have lost sight of miracles?

CHAPTER SIX

Miracles: The Gift of the Holy Life to a Less Holy World

1. Why are *miracles* called the "gift of a holy life"?

2. Why is *humility* called the "gift of seeing our importance next to God's"?

3. Who was Anthony of the Desert's most formidable foe? How did he overcome him?

4. How did the terms *transubstantiation* and *breakfast* originate?

5. Why is *asceticism* called the "force of miracle"?

6. What does the term *mortification* mean? How does it help in bringing the power of miracle to the Christian's life?

7. What does it mean to say that those who live consecrated lives not only work miracles, but they make possible the continuance of the race?

CHAPTER SEVEN

Do Miracles Still Happen and What Difference Does it Make?

1. What is a *relic*? Why are they important to some Christians? How did Luther feel about them? Augustine?

2. What is meant by "the power of the name"?

3. Why do Catholics seem to have less trouble believing in miracles than Protestants?

4. What are the *stigmata*? How would you relate this idea to Galatians 2:20?

CHAPTER EIGHT

Exorcisms: Christ's Most Important Miracles

1. Why are Christ's exorcisms thought to be his most significant miracles?

2. Why are exorcisms referred to as "the high work of holiness"?
3. Who does Scott Peck designate as "people of the lie"?
4. What does the term *other kingdom* mean?
5. Name two of the categories of demons and express why you think this kind of possession would be severe. Are all cases of possession mental illness? Why or why not?

CHAPTER NINE

Miracles: God's Way of Saying We Matter

1. How are miracles God's reply to our meaninglessness?
2. How do miracles prove we count with God?
3. What did Viktor Frankl mean by "meaning therapy"?
4. What did Neuhauster mean when he said that not to believe in miracles paves the way to the annihilation of life?
5. What was Helen Keller's "detonation of life"? How can the idea be applied to us?

CHAPTER TEN

The Final Wonder: The World on Fire

1. What is the greatest biblical miracle yet unperformed? Why is it spoken of in this way?
2. What are some evidences we are "slouching toward Sodom"?
4. Draw a connection between apocalypse and hope.
5. How did Paul's view of apocalypse change as he got older?

EPILOGUE

Miracles: Whether We Understand Them or Not, the Least We Can Do Is Try to Celebrate Them

1. What does it mean to say miracles supply us with a deeper yearning than we know?

2. What does it mean to say that miracles happen whether we see them or not?

Notes

1. Cookie Bakke, from *Mensa Bulletin*, May 1999. mensabull@aol.com.
2. Calvin Miller, *The Book of Jesus* (NY: Simon & Schuster, 1996) p. 284.
3. *Henry V*, IV, vii.
4. Marjorie L. Kimbrough, *Everyday Miracles* (Nashville: Dimensions for Living, 1997) pp. 13–14.
5. Calvin Miller, *A Hunger for Meaning* (Downers Grove, IL: Inter-Varsity Press, 1984) p. 35.
6. Michael Arvey, *Miracles* (San Diego, CA: Greenhaven Press, Inc., 1990) p. 93–94.
7. Michael Arvey, *Miracles* (San Diego, CA: Greenhaven Press, Inc., 1990) p. 95.
8. Michael Arvey, *Miracles* (San Diego, CA: Greenhaven Press, Inc., 1990) p. 96.
9. Erich von Däniken, *Miracles of the Gods*, (NY: Delacorte Press, 1974) p. 125.
10. Joan Wester Anderson, *Where Miracles Happen* (NY: Brett Books, Inc., 1994) pp. 15–16.
11. Calvin Miller, *A Hunger for Meaning* (Downers Grove, IL: InterVarsity Press, 1984) pp. 98–100.
12. Douglas Connelly, *Miracles* (Downers Grove, IL: InterVarsity Press, 1997) p. 15.
13. Michael Arvey, *Miracles* (San Diego, CA: Greenhaven Press, Inc., 1990) p. 52.
14. Charles Wesley, *Hark! The Herald Angels Sing*, taken from *The Baptist Hymnal* (Nashville, TN: Convention Press, 1975 edition) p. 83.
15. Calvin Miller, *The Singer* (Downers Grove, IL: InterVarsity Press, 2001) p. 103.

16. Calvin Miller, *The Singer* (Downers Grove, IL: InterVarsity Press, 2001) p. 103.
17. Douglas Connelly, *Miracles* (Downers Grove, IL: InterVarsity Press, 1997) p. 53.
18. Douglas Connelly, *Miracles* (Downers Grove, IL: InterVarsity Press, 1997) p. 60.
19. Calvin Miller, *A Hunger for Meaning* (Downers Grove, IL: Inter-Varsity Press, 1984) p. 83.
20. King Lear, V, iii
21. Calvin Miller, *A Hunger for Meaning* (Downers Grove, IL: InterVarsity Press, 1984) p. 83.
22. Ibid, p. 84.
23. Ibid.
24. Ibid.
25. Ibid, p. 85.
26. Ibid.
27. Ibid, pp. 85–86.
28. Joan Wester Anderson, *Where Miracles Happen* (NY: Brett Books, Inc., 1994) p. 78.
29. Joan Wester Anderson, *Where Miracles Happen* (NY: Brett Books, Inc., 1994) p. 84.
30. Joan Wester Anderson, *Where Miracles Happen* (NY: Brett Books, Inc., 1994) p. 154.
31. Erich Von Däniken, *Miracles of the Gods* (NY: Delacorte Press, 1974) p. 109.
32. J. B. Phillips, *Ring of Truth*, (London: Hodder and Stoughton, 1967) pp 89–90.
33. G. K. Chesterton, *Orthodoxy* (San Francisco: St. Ignatius Press, 1995).
34. John Milner, *The Life of St. Francis Xavier* (Philadelphia: The Society of Jesus, 1841) p.112.
35. Robert Bruce Mullin, *Miracles and the Modern Religious Imagination* (New Haven, Connecticut: Yale University Press, 1996) pp.105–106.
36. Douglas Connelly, *Miracles* (Downers Grove, IL: InterVarsity Press, 1997) p. 103.
37. Leo Tolstoy, *The Memoirs of a Madman* as quoted in *The Book of Jesus*, edited by Calvin Miller (NY: Simon & Schuster, 1996) p. 523.
38. Kenneth L. Woodward, *The Book of Miracles* (NY: Touchstone, 2000) p. 169.

39. As quoted in Joe Nickell, *Looking for a Miracle* (NY: Prometheus Books, 1993), pp. 118–119.
40. Kenneth L. Woodward, *The Book of Miracles* (NY: Touchstone, 2000) p. 81.
41. Douglas Connelly, *Miracles* (Downers Grove, IL: InterVarsity Press, 1997) p. 12.
42. Kenneth L. Woodward, *The Book of Miracles* (NY: Touchstone, 2000) p. 15.
43. Keith Thomas, *Religion and the Decline of Magic* (Oxford: Oxford Univ. Press. 1971) pp. 30–31.
44. Kenneth L. Woodward, *The Book of Miracles* (NY: Touchstone, 2000) pp. 157–158.
45. Calvin Miller, several paragraphs above footnote are taken from *A Hunger for Meaning* (Downers Grove, IL: InterVarsity Press, 1984.
46. Kenneth L. Woodward, *The Book of Miracles* (NY: Touchstone, 2000) p. 26.
47. Douglas Connelly, *Miracles* (Downers Grove, IL: InterVarsity Press, 1997) p. 14.
48. Keith Thomas, *Religion and the Decline of Magic* (Oxford: Oxford Univ. Press, 1971) pp. 297–301.
49. Douglas Connelly, *Miracles* (Downers Grove, IL: InterVarsity, 1997) p. 46.
50. Kenneth L. Woodward, *The Book of Miracles* (NY: Touchstone, 2000) p. 168.
51. Douglas Connelly, *Miracles* (Downers Grove, IL: InterVarsity, 1997) p. 73.
52. Kenneth L. Woodward, *The Book of Miracles* (NY: Touchstone, 2000) p. 154.
53. Kenneth L. Woodward, *The Book of Miracles* (NY: Touchstone, 2000) p. 155.
54. Calvin Miller, Much of these recent pages occurred in part in *A Hunger for Meaning* (Downers Grove, IL: InterVarsity Press, 1984) pp. 108–113.
55. The material in the previous paragraphs appeared in a similar form in *A Hunger for Meaning* (Downers Grove, IL: InterVarsity Press, 1984).
56. The material in these paragraphs are in a similar form in *A Hunger for Meaning* (Downers Grove, IL: InterVarsity Press, 1984).

57. Joan Wester Anderson, *Where Miracles Happen* (NY: Brett Books, Inc., 1994) pp. 25–27.
58. This story is a similar one first printed in Calvin Miller's *A Hunger for Meaning* (Downers Grove, IL: InterVarsity Press, 1984) pp. 40–41.
59. *The Second Coming*, Jan. 1919
60. *Locksley Hall*, lines 119-ff.
61. Judith Deem Dupree, *We shall Hear* as quoted in *The Book of Jesus*, edited by Calvin Miller (NY: Simon & Schuster, 1996) p. 612.
62. George Vandeman, *Planet In Rebellion* (: Pacific Press, 19—)
63. Judith Deem Dupree, *I Sing America* (Pine Valley, CA: Quiddity Press, 2002) p. 13.